START
to
RIDE

START
—to—
RIDE

Holger Heck and Volker Greiner
Translated by Chris Belton

J.A. Allen
London

British Library Cataloguing in Publication Data

Heck, Holger
    Start to ride.
    I. Title   II. Greiner, Volker
    III. Schritt, trab, galopp. *English*
    798.23
    ISBN 0851315364

First published in Germany in 1987 by BLV Verlagsgesellschaft mbH, Munchen

Published in Great Britain in 1991 by
J.A. Allen & Company Limited,
1 Lower Grosvenor Place, London SW1W 0EL.

© English translation, J.A. Allen & Company Limited, 1991

Designed by Nancy Lawrence
Additional material by Martin Diggle and Maggie Raynor

Typeset in Hong Kong by Setrite Typesetters Ltd.
Printed in Hong Kong by Dah Hua Printing Co. Ltd.

Contents

Contents

Introduction

Who Can Ride?

'I can ride', says the girl. During their last holiday in Spain, her parents paid for her to have an hour's ride every couple of days on a placid little grey horse. The girl managed to stay on the quiet, well-mannered horse very well, and the day before they came home she even coped with a long hack along the beach with some other riders. What the girl means is, 'I have sat on a horse a few times'. Of course, she cannot really ride.

The distinguished old riding master dismounts from his horse following a breathtaking display of advanced dressage. He rubs his head on his sleeve and says, 'A lifetime is not long enough to learn how to ride'. Yet he can ride, can't he? Of course he can, but what he is saying is that learning to ride is not like learning to use a machine. Once you have mastered the use of all the knobs and levers, you can work a machine — one person is as good at it as the next, but when you are dealing with horses, you learn something new every day, and gain more understanding.

The old riding master might also say, 'I can train most horses, and can present trained horses under saddle to the best of their abilities, but there are also horses to whom I cannot do justice; horses with whom, with my skills, I cannot deal'.

'Being able to ride' is therefore relative. Riding is an art. Yet, as with all arts, the rider starts in a small, amateur way; in the same way that small children start painting in the kindergarten. Even in these early stages, one child will show more imagination, more sensitivity, and even more skill than another. Whether or not they can paint is a question which is impossible to answer. Rembrandt, Picasso and Chagall painted, but could they paint? The answer must certainly be yes. But which of them was best? Again, the question is impossible to answer because styles, interpretations, and the ways in which a work of art is created are too varied.

Did Picasso, for example, ever reach the stage where there was nothing more to be learned? He would have

laughed at such a suggestion, and would perhaps have replied, 'In art, you never stop learning'.

This is exactly what the old riding master meant when he said, 'A lifetime is not long enough to learn how to ride'.

We must make a clear distinction between being able to ride, and sitting on a trained horse which does more or less what is asked of it. In order to sit on a trained horse and ride school figures, or enjoy a hack in the country, all that is necessary is the ability and body control to give a few well-rehearsed aids. Being able to ride, in the true sense of the expression, requires another quality, because this is where the art begins. There is no question that, first and foremost, the

foundations must be laid. Without a craftsman's knowledge of colour composition, paintbrushes, perspective, and different techniques, not even Picasso would have been able to become a great painter. He became a great master, an artist, yet millions of people learn the craft upon which his artistry is based.

First, then, the craft must be learned, but with the clear understanding that it is the starting point on the road to the art. The rider will progress and be able to aspire to be an artist only if he understands this from the outset, and does not think after six months' training, when he has acquired some measure of security in the saddle, that this means that he can ride. It must also be made clear that although the craft is within the scope of anyone, physical capabilities, but above all talent and sensitivity, are necessary for an artist, and will distinguish the artist from the craftsman.

This book does not pretend to be a work on equitation in the classical sense. It begins with the first visit to the riding school, and finishes at the point where the rider can sit relatively securely in the saddle in walk, trot and canter. Its aim is, therefore, to give the rider practical help in achieving a secure and independent seat in the saddle in the three gaits.

It is annoying, and suggestive of laziness and thoughtlessness, when riding instructors continually recommend studies on classical equitation to beginners. Major Wilhelm Mueseler is one of the most important writers on the theory of equitation of the present century. His *Riding Logic* is a masterpiece on the subject of classical horsemanship; it is, however, quite unsuitable for a complete beginner. Mueseler did not intend it for the beginner, but for the expert, like Picasso writing to

Chagall. Every attempt has been made in this book to avoid technical horsey terminology. The text can be understood by any logical-minded person, and is supported and lucidly illustrated by the splendid drawings provided by Volker Greiner. Just as in early driving lessons – clutch in, put it into gear, then gradually let the clutch out – it is easy once you know how; you can do it without even thinking. But how difficult it seems when you simply cannot get the hang of it, and the car is leaping about like a bucking bronco.

The same thing happens with riding. Once the initial hurdles have been overcome, you have understood which aids do what, and when to use them, and once you have found your balance, everything will become easier, and you will gradually make more and more progress. A good rider no longer thinks about which aids to use while he is on the horse – he (almost) always uses the right aids instinctively. The beginner will not achieve this by practice alone. There are only two ways to do so; either the rider has instinctive feel and sensitivity, or, to begin with, he focuses his mind on the action and effects of his aids, and learns as he rides how his actions, and their varying levels of intensity, influence the horse.

It is with this introductory process that this book aims to help. If you understand what the rider means to the horse, you will understand the true meaning of the last sentence: this beginners' instruction book has been written primarily for the horse.

Brand-Hof, 1987   Holger Heck

1

What is a Horse?

How Our Horses Have Evolved

Is man descended from the ape? Or does he have his own evolutionary history? A question for anthropologists perhaps. However, we do know that man has not always looked like he does today, and has not always existed in this form; he has evolved to his present form. Examination of the suits of armour of the knights of the Middle Ages shows that man has grown taller, and in only a few centuries. Similarly, horses have not always looked as they do today; they too have a long evolutionary history behind them.

It is estimated that there are about 40 million horses in the world, and about 300 different breeds.

For about 5,000 years, the horse has been a domesticated animal, helping man with his work, carrying him to war, providing him with meat, and giving him enjoyment in his leisure time.

2

The Horse Comes From the Forest

Nowadays, when we speak of 'wild horses', we mean the ancestors of our present-day horses. There are a few of these wild horses left, living and grazing on the steppes and savannas, and in human terms they could be compared to grandparents rather than parents of the modern horse. Even the legendary Equus Przewalski (named after his Russian discoverer), might be better compared to a great-grand-parent.

From bone discoveries, it has been possible to establish that the so-called Przewalski's horse was already in existence about a million years ago.

However, the first animals which can be counted as ancestors of the modern horse were roaming the earth 40 million years ago. Even if there had been humans on the earth at this time, it would never have occurred to them to climb onto this animal's back and ride it — that is, not unless they were midgets — because the earliest ancestors of the modern horse were not much bigger than a small dog. Scientists named these small horses Eohippus, but we can only surmise what they actually looked like; for example, they probably had hairy coats. What is certain is that they lived

Eohippus,   Mesohippus,   Merychippus, in the woods and fed mainly on leaves. At that time the earth was covered almost completely with woods, seas, lakes and enormous patches of ice. Over millions of years it changed; the ice patches gradually became smaller and finally disappeared except for two small areas — the Arctic and Antarctic. The climate also changed, becoming warmer gradually. Forests gave way to more open landscape. The early horses adapted to their changing habitat. This evolution lasted about 25 to 30 million years. For about the last 10 million years, the horse, no longer a forest dweller, has been a grazing animal and inhabitant of the steppes.

The modern horse is now classified as a soliped, or single-toed animal, but it has not always been so. About 20 million years ago the horse still had three toes, and only started to walk on one toe about five million years ago. The other, vestigial, toes can still be seen, for example the 'chestnut', near the hock joint, and the so-called splint bones. The latter are bones on the inside of the cannon bone, which is the lower part of the horse's leg, below the knee and above the foot. The splint bone no longer has any function.

The Horse as the Hunter's Prey

Many thinkers and philosophers consider the wheel to be man's most important discovery. Similarly, we might consider how much imagination was needed to come up with the idea that an animal's pulling power and movement could be harnessed and put to use, because, at first, the horse was simply prey to be hunted down and eaten.

It was probably in the Orient that the horse was first harnessed to a vehicle, and it was many years before man first sat on his back. The first people to achieve mounted status did so 1,200 years before Christ.

Pliohippus,

Equus Przewalski

The Evolution of the Different Breeds

The 50 million years of the horse's evolution did not, of course, take place along one single path. It branched off in many different directions. Zebras and donkeys are two examples of these branches; others are the different types and breeds of horse. For example, the only thing an Arabian has in common with a heavy, Belgian warmblood is the species. What we now know as breeds were at first only different types. It was under man's influence that these different types became established and were refined as breeds, with their different characteristics clearly defined.

We should not, however, imagine that horse breeding in its present form has existed for hundreds of years. Horses were not normally bred as status symbols, but primarily as replacements for existing horses which were no longer fit for work or war.

It was the use for which the horse was intended, and of course its environment, which decided the course of the horse's development over the generations. German horse breeders, even today, say that a horse is the product of the soil on which it is reared. It is not only the actual soil to which they are referring, but the whole of the horse's habitat: the ground he uses for exercise and on which his food grows, the climate, and all the other natural phenomena which influence him.

In mountainous regions with a very harsh climate, small tough horses with hard feet have developed, whilst in flat regions with lush, juicy grass, but heavy, deep soil, the horses which

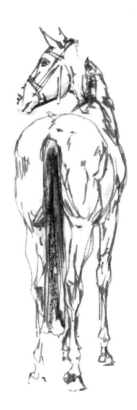

have evolved are bigger, heavier, a bit coarser and somewhat less active.

In recent years, these differences have gradually diminished, and the influence of habitat on the development of the horse has become less significant. Firstly, since horses are no longer confined to their own region of origin, breeding stock and riding horses from far distant places intermingle. Secondly, it is now possible to feed horses everywhere with the same food.

Most horse-breeding countries all over the world now have breed societies, the majority of which were set up after the Second World War. The breeders got together to establish a common objective and to form a body which would represent their common interest.

3

The Horse is a Monster!

The horse is a monster which kicks at one end and bites at the other! This is the sort of thing people say when they want to emphasise that they are not involved with horses and riding. Similarly, people who do not like football call it a silly game in which 22 grown men run around kicking a ball.

The horse strikes the layman as being relatively large, and this visual

impression of size inspires respect, and sometimes fear. This is understandable. A person who is not used to animals is much less afraid of a small animal such as a dachshund or a cat, to whom he is not inferior in physical strength; he has to watch out for their teeth and claws, but that is all.

It only takes a few riding lessons for the beginner to realise that the horse's size and his controllability are totally unrelated. Almost every student of riding is relieved at first if he is allocated the smallest horse; the others look so big! Yet an unruly pony can cause the rider far more problems than a big, well-behaved school horse, and the risk of injury is the same whether you fall off an 8 h.h. pony or a 17 h.h. horse. The height of a horse or pony is measured in hands (h.h.), 1 h.h. = 4 in, and the measurement is taken at the animal's withers (base of the neck).

The horse is a creature of flight; a fact that is instilled into riders during their first few lessons, yet this expression on its own is meaningless. Every living creature has 'weapons' and defences with which to protect himself against dangers which threaten his well-being or life. A tiger has his silent step, his agility, his teeth and claws. The main defence of the horse, and of every creature of flight, is his speed, and, therefore, the ability to escape from his enemy.

Speed is the horse's most effective defence, and consequently his first choice. It is true that he also has teeth and hooves with which he can defend himself, yet it is obvious that these weapons will not be used unless absolutely necessary, since they are not very effective against his natural foes in the wild. The horse's teeth are blunt, and designed to chew grass, and, in spite of his size, a horse can rarely defeat a lion or tiger with his hooves. Hence the first reaction of any sound, healthy horse is to run away.

Before a dog bites, he gives plenty of warning of his intentions. First of all the hair on his back and neck stands on end. Then he starts to growl quietly and curl his lips. Only when he has done this will he finally bite. A horse uses his defences in a similar way, only in reverse. At the first sign of danger he runs away. He does not do so out of cowardice but because the move is a sound and sensible one in the light of his capabilities. A horse must always be on his guard in order to save his life. When a horse who has been lying down asleep in his box overnight, suddenly stands up when someone goes in, this is the first reaction to a situation from which it may be necessary to run away. When a horse panics on feeling a saddle unexpectedly thrown on his back, this is the same sort of reaction; a preparation for flight. The novice rider must constantly bear this in mind. If the horse tries to dash away, this is usually a perfectly natural reaction.

Horses are herd animals. Nature created them this way on purpose. When an animal's best defence is flight from a possible enemy, he needs the added protection afforded by others of his own kind keeping a lookout. Every horse has to sleep some time. How can he keep watch when he is asleep? Horses in a herd take it in turns to stand guard; some sleep, but there are always some standing guard.

In office or community life there must be someone in charge, otherwise there is chaos. The same applies to a herd. In every herd of horses, even today, there is a clearly defined pecking order; every horse knows his place. Naturally, the horse at the top of the pecking order has the most responsibility, the most work, in the herd, therefore this is the first horse to eat and drink. Even when horses are together only in the stables, and are

[10]

never allowed out together in the field — as happens in most riding stables — this pecking order still evolves. It is noticeable that this top horse in the 'stable herd' is the last one to lie down at night, and the first to get up when someone goes into the stables in the morning.

Flight and the herd: these are the two things which mean survival to horses. They have retained an instinctive knowledge of this, despite the fact that conditions and influences have changed completely.

We make use of these two very essential instincts both when we are handling and looking after horses, and when we are riding them. Sometimes, however, we have to guide these instincts a little in the right direction if we are to obtain the desired result. For example, a young horse must learn that when he is being ridden he will have to leave the other horses, but that later he will be allowed to return to them. So, when we are training a young horse, we take an older, experienced horse along, and place him in the lead. The young horse will follow the older one trustingly, and learn in this way that nothing awful is going to happen to him. In this example, on the one hand, the herd instinct must be overcome — so that, later, the horse will go out by himself — but on the other hand, it is exploited during the early stages — with the older, escort horse.

The horse is not a dog. This is so obvious as to sound silly, yet most people tend to compare an animal they do not know with one they do know. There is, however, virtually nothing in equine behaviour which can be compared with canine behaviour. Every beginner will be surprised at how, in the early stages, he keeps treating the horse like a dog, and expecting him to behave like one.

Normally — and the few exceptions cannot be substantiated — a horse cannot recognise his name. He remembers voices and tones of voice, but cannot recognise even a simple name, never mind something like Ibn Abba Sherif Pasha! Whatever the name, it is all the same to the horse. What does matter is the tone used, and horses are very sensitive to the difference between a reproving and a calming voice. The worst punishment for a horse consists of being shouted at. In many cases, an overwrought stallion can be brought back under control more successfully by speaking loudly to him than by hitting him. It is not what you say to a horse, but how you say it, which is important.

As a creature of flight, the horse is, therefore, an animal which needs exercise. If he cannot exercise, he becomes ill. He can be compared with a car which is not used; he goes rusty.

In the wild, horses are almost always moving about, if only in walk. They spend only a few hours each day lying down, or dozing in a standing position. They have to move around constantly to obtain their food, taking mouthfuls of grass, step by step, as they go. Horses kept in stables in the modern way tend to have their meals placed before them — cut and dried as it were — and their movement restricted. It follows that many horses today are not kept in conditions suited to their species. This is how it has to be, and, in most cases, however much we love our animals, there is nothing we can do about it.

Since this is the case, however, the comparatively short time that the horse is being ridden must be used to advantage, and the horse exercised correctly. As far as possible, work under saddle must compensate for the unsuitable living conditions. To get back to our engine which has been left standing for some time, when it is first started up, it should only be run at low R.P.M. (revolutions per minute) to start with, and not at full throttle. Similarly, a horse must progress to hard work gradually.

Horses are herbivores, and nowadays, they are fed partly on carefully balanced food mixes. The necessary minerals, trace elements and vitamins have already been added to the feed. Basically, however, the horse's diet is made up of two main components: concentrated food (traditionally, oats) and forage (traditionally, grass or hay). In addition, a horse weighing, for example, 450 to 600 kg. needs approximately 20 to 30 l. of water per day.

[13]

4

What is a Rider?

All Horses Think: 'Down with Riders!'

If it were up to the horses, there would be no riders. Horses enjoy eating, they enjoy running around in the field and like rolling in the sand, but carrying a rider is not something they do for fun.

Many horses whinny when their rider comes into the stable. People often say this is because the horse is pleased that he is going to be ridden. However, this is not quite true. The horse gives a joyful whinny because the rider often comes bearing titbits. He is pleased that someone has come to talk to him, or because he knows that he is going to be let out of his stable to get some exercise. The fact that at the same time there will be a rider on his back can only be construed by him as a necessary evil.

An animal-lover might interpret this to mean that horses should not be ridden because they do not want to be ridden. If they had any say in the matter, the horses would applaud this interpretation, but it is the same as saying that all factory conveyor belts should be switched off because most of the operators would prefer to go home and amuse themselves.

In all sectors of our lives we have to make compromises, even on the subject of our horses' well-being. If the riding of horses were banned, the eventual result would be that the only place left in which to admire them would be the zoo. Why would people keep and breed horses if they could not use them? This might be acceptable with a small animal, because the costs involved would be considerably lower, and the time required would be less. After all, in times of financial crisis, when something has to go, will it be the guard-dog, or will it be the poodle, which is simply a luxury?

An animal must, therefore, serve some useful purpose if the conservation of the species is to be assured. The role of partner to man in sport and leisure is a very important one for the horse.

But why do horses not like being ridden? This is a very simple question to answer: nature did not plan it that way. The horse was not designed, from the point of view of skeleton or build, to carry a man, and is not equipped for it like a car, which even has seats provided.

If someone sits on your shoulders, you only need to take a few steps with the extra weight on top to realise how it must feel for the horse to carry a rider on his back. The first steps are hesitant, because you must first find your balance again. As time goes on, you get used to it and gradually become steadier. The position of your centre of gravity alters, owing to the additional weight, and you must first get used to its new position.

It is the same for the horse, except that the horse cannot understand this from a short explanation, he must come to understand it through lengthy exercises. At first, the rider is simply a foreign body on his back. A trained horse has learned to balance this external, and even moving, weight on his back, but it takes young horses months or, sometimes, even years to find this new balance, and so become 'in balance' as it is called by the riding fraternity. However, one further, and possibly even more important, psychological factor is relevant here; the horse can run away from its enemy, but he has little defence against an animal which jumps onto his back. So predators such as lions, tend to jump onto a horse's back and sink their teeth into the base of the neck. The horse runs away, but is usually unable to shake off his enemy — he runs till he drops. In circuses, the act in which a tiger rides on the back of a horse is a particularly difficult one for which to train.

A young horse must, therefore, get used to the extra weight, and at the same time overcome his instinctive fear of something on his back. Most horses try to run away the first time the rider gets on their back, and when they realise that they cannot get rid of the rider by rushing forwards, some then go backwards. There are even those who try to throw themsleves to the ground to shake off the unaccustomed weight from their back.

An older horse has learned gradually that there is nothing to fear from the rider on his back, but this does not mean that he has lost the instinct to flee; only that a good trainer has put that instinct to good use. The horse's first reaction to the pressure brought to bear by the bracing of the rider's back muscles or the application of his lower leg, is to try to escape. This he does by going forwards. In the course of his training, the horse learns to interpret these actions by the rider as signals, but for this to happen he must lose the logical nervousness which he experiences at first. This is achieved by tactful, sensitive use of the voice, the hands and the body aids. Only then can the trainer begin slowly to make it clear to the horse that he is trying to obtain a specific reaction when he presses his legs against the horse's sides, or carefully picks up the reins.

This short explanation should make it clear that horsemanship, correctly practised, has nothing to do with force. Rider and horse, after a long period of training together, must be in harmony. A rider heavily armed with spurs, whip, strong biceps, and thigh muscles which work like a giant pair of pincers, is not setting out to establish harmony between horse and rider, but rather to engage in a battle of which, in the long run, he can only be the loser.

5

Which Rider for Which Horse?

There is an old German saying which states: 'It is on an old nag that you learn how to ride'. The saying does not really apply specifically to riders; all it means is that a pupil learns from an experienced teacher, but it does, however, also apply to riding. A beginner should be put on an experienced horse, and young horses should be trained by experienced riders.

A horse which is to be ridden by a beginner must be able to do all the things that the rider has to learn at this stage, otherwise things will not work out.

Ideally a schoolmaster should be used. 'Schoolmaster' is a term used by horsemen to denote an experienced riding horse who will help the rider progress. In some riding establishments, ex-competition horses are used for school work, when, for example, they may have become too old to compete. Given moderate work these horses certainly continue to earn their keep.

A schoolmaster recognises a correctly applied aid and will only respond if the aids *are* correctly applied and coordinated; an inaccurate aid will receive no response. The rider learns from the instructor what aids to use, and in what intensity, to make the horse respond. Thus the rider learns the aids precisely and relatively quickly.

The schoolmaster is also quiet and tolerant, and is used to beginners on his back. He has to be tolerant because,

naturally, a learner rider will do a lot of things wrong for a long time.

Anyone who has a chance to ride such a horse should do so, as often as possible, because there is nothing better than an experienced horse for teaching the novice to ride.

Nowadays, when we talk about cruelty to animals, it is not the brutal bully who is the biggest threat. Cruelty due to an inability to cope, and to ignorance, is far more common. It is not malicious or intentional, but it causes the animal just as much suffering. Many a poor dog is 'fed to death' by a so-called animal-lover, some lonely person who, out of ignorance and an exaggerated and misguided love for the animal, gives it a chocolate here, the remains of the cutlet there. It is a very sad reflection on modern society that this loneliness exists, but it does not change the fact that the animals are the victims of cruelty.

Horses also have to suffer a great deal which is due to the ignorance of the person looking after, or riding, them. The rider must understand clearly that no other domesticated animal has to endure such a close physical contact with man over a long period. A dog, a cat, and even a bird, can escape from displays of affection which they find annoying. A horse can rarely get rid of his rider; he has to tolerate him. This contact begins

[17]

with the weight which the rider places in the saddle. A big, strong warmblood horse can carry about 90 kg. without any great problem. Anybody who is heavier than this should give up riding, or lose weight – not only for the good of the horse. However, even below this 90 kg. threshold, the rider's weight still has to be taken into account. A person weighing 80 kg. has no business to be riding a dainty, finely-built horse in the early stages of training. Training a horse does not just mean teaching it to understand the rider's aids. The muscles, tendons and ligaments concerned must also be developed and strengthened. For example, a correctly trained horse has strong, well-developed muscles running along his back, so that he can, at least temporarily, carry a heavy rider without sustaining any permanent injury to his spine.

When it comes to selecting a mount, a wide variety of different horse and pony types is available to choose from, ranging from the 40 in. high Shetland to the 18 h.h. Shire horse.

For riders between 50 kg. and 70 kg. in weight, a big horse like this is not really suitable. However, a strong horse should be available for riders over 70 kg. in weight (if used for beginners, it should also be well schooled); these horses are known as weight-carriers.

All riders, before their first lesson, will try to make contact with the horse upon which they will shortly be sitting. 'I'm giving him a pat so he knows I like him and then he won't throw me.' Beginner riders seem to think this is some kind of insurance policy! There are two things which single out the good student from the start: he should try to have as much contact with the horse as possible (grooming, stroking etc.), and he should be determined to learn to ride well.

However, not too much should be expected from this early contact. It would not be realistic to do so. A school horse is ridden by three, four, five, or even six, different riders every day. He loves them all, they all bring him a titbit and give him a pat. In this respect too he grows indifferent.

Moreover, once on his back, the rider is a completely different being from the one the horse met in the stable. Humans would react to each other the same way in a similar situation, for example, a person will pull out all the stops to help his best friend, even if it inconveniences him. However, when he is playing tennis against him, he will do everything the rules allow to beat him; he will not once send the ball the wrong way to benefit his opponent. In the stable, the horse enjoys the pats, and does not have to be asked twice to eat the titbits, but he will try to get this same person off his back when he gets fed up with him. This does not mean that the horse has something personal against the rider, but he objects to the clumsy aids, the weight — which is like a sack of potatoes on his back — the whip, or the spurs.

The majority of horses stand still immediately they have unseated their riders — just as if nothing had happened. As far as they are concerned, nothing much *has* happened, they have simply stated, in their own way, 'I didn't understand you, you said the wrong thing'.

You cannot make the horse understand that it makes a difference to the rider whether the horse simply shakes his head angrily, or whether he puts the rider on the floor. In both cases the horse is trying to say that he is being treated wrongly, but only the rider knows the difference; if he hits the ground, it hurts. However, the horse does not change his behaviour towards the rider as a result of having bucked him off.

It is an unfortunate fact that, nowadays, many riders do not know much about horses, but there are various reasons for this failing. In days gone by, it was mainly farmers' sons, big landowners, and soldiers serving in the cavalry, who rode horses. These were people who had grown up with horses — there had been horsemen in their families for generations; the grandfather had passed on his knowledge to the father, and the father to the son.

People who ride today have not usually been brought up with the sound of horses whinnying in the paddock outside the nursery window. They are townspeople, people who, at some point in their lives, have felt drawn towards these magnificent creatures. Among them are people who own a horse because they consider it socially desirable. There are many riders in this category; they get on the horse, which is ready-groomed and saddled, do a few circuits of the school, and then go off, feeling much better. These people enjoy their riding, but will never become horsemen.

after just four, five or eight years, when, perhaps for the first thirty years of his life, he has had no contact with them?

A person with the right physical attributes and the necessary 'feel' can go a long way with his riding in a few years, and can have numerous trophies on his mantelpiece, yet he still does not understand any more about horses than it is possible to learn in four, five or eight years, and that is not very much.

For most people, riding remains a hobby, for which there is never enough time, but to understand horses, and be able to analyse and assess them, a great deal of experience is needed. This can only be gained by dealing with very many horses over a long period of time.

We must get away from the idea that all the famous riders are good horse-masters, and know a lot about horses. Some are excellent in this respect, but some are not so good. Some will recognise a good horse as soon as he puts his head over the door, others will pass by a 'top prospect' (a horse with talent and potential) without a second glance.

If, for a person who has spent all his life with horses, a lifetime is not enough to learn all there is to know about them, what chance does a person have of knowing a lot about horses

6

The Riding School

Laymen, and those new to riding, may be confused by the various terms used to describe places where horses are kept. In order to avoid time-wasting and perhaps embarrassment on the part of the newcomers seeking somewhere to ride, we should first clarify these terms.

A 'stud' is an establishment primarily concerned with the breeding of horses, usually of a specific breed (Thoroughbred, Arab and so on) or 'type' (warmblood, performance horses, riding ponies). While the former concentrate on perpetuating bloodlines (that is to say, a Thoroughbred stud will normally produce pure-bred foals from pure-bred parents), the latter will often 'blend' the qualities of different breeds in an attempt to produce stock whose composite characteristics make them particularly suitable for certain activities, such as show-jumping or dressage.

Although the word 'stud' can be used to describe a place where both stallions and mares are kept permanently, or, indeed, where mares are kept permanently and 'visited' by stallions, it is now most commonly used to describe a permanent base for stallions, to whom mares are sent temporarily to be 'covered'. In Britain, virtually all studs are privately owned and, although the occupants will be ridden or exercised according to their needs, they will not be used to provide tuition for the public, nor would they normally be suitable for this purpose.

A 'livery yard' is an establishment which derives income from looking after horses on behalf of their owners. Although they sometimes offer tuition to these owners, specialist livery yards do not normally offer it to the public; they could hardly use the privately-owned horses for this purpose and, even if they have a few suitable horses of their own, they tend to avoid the risk of conflict over use of facilities for which the livery owners effectively pay. Occasionally, however, establishments operate both a livery yard and a riding school (usually, the more separate they are kept, the better), and many riding schools have a few horses — usually owned by established clients — at livery.

'Stable' is simply the traditional name for a building used to accommodate a horse. Thus 'stable block' refers to a group of such buildings, and 'stable yard' usually defines a stable block with some associated amenities. In practice, 'stables' is commonly used to refer loosely to any place where horses are accommodated, and a phrase incorporating this word may not fully define the purpose for which the stabled horses are used. For example, a 'riding stable' may be, in part, a riding school, or it may be simply a place from which horses can be hired to 'hack out' (ride in the open). Whatever qualities they may possess, these latter are not suitable for beginners and, indeed, reputable hacking stables will not knowingly entertain such clients, since they will acknowledge that, in the interests of all, the basics of riding should first be learnt under instruction in an enclosed arena.

For most people this learning — and perhaps learning well beyond the basics — will take place in a riding school. This, by definition, is an establishment whose primary purpose is to provide riding instruction, although some perform this task a good deal better than others. For anyone unable to act upon personal recommendation, finding a suitable riding school may take a little time and effort, but this will prove well worthwhile.

In Britain, it is a statutory requirement (1970 Riding Establishments Act) that establishments hiring out horses in connection with instruction for financial reward must be licensed by the Local Authority, subject to satisfying the requirements of an annual inspection. The fundamental guideline for anyone seeking a riding school is, then, that it should be so licensed, and a list of licensed schools should be available from the Recreation or Amenities Department of the Local Authority concerned. However, although the requirements of the Riding Establishments Act are generally relevant in terms of equine welfare, public health considerations and safety, possession of a licence does not really guarantee the quality of instruction available. More useful guidance in this respect is the approval of a riding school by the British Horse Society (B.H.S.) and/or the Association of British Riding Schools (A.B.R.S.).

The object of the B.H.S. is to promote the interests of equines and improve the standards of riding and horsemastership nationally. To these ends, it is generally responsible for much of the organisation and promotion of riding in Britain, and administers a series of professional exams for riding instructors. The A.B.R.S. is, in essence, a trade association of riding school proprietors, and one way in which it protects the interests of its members is by seeking to ensure that their establishments are well run.

Both these bodies carry out annual inspections of licensed schools associated with them, and confer their own approvals where appropriate. Although each have slightly different criteria, these are generally additional to the statutory requirements, and place a greater emphasis on teaching standards.

While there is no legal requirement for a licensed riding school to be inspected by, or even involved with, these bodies, it is generally considered that their approvals enhance the status of a school, and thus many seek such approval in their own interests. A school approved by the B.H.S. will

display a blue plaque to that effect, stating the year of approval (which should be current), and a school which has passed the A.B.R.S. inspection will have an A.B.R.S. Member sign on display. Details of such schools can be obtained respectively from: B.H.S. Bookshop, National Equestrian Centre, Stoneleigh, Warks., and, A.B.R.S., Old Brewery Yard, Penzance, Cornwall.

Returning to the definition of terms, it will be apparent from literature provided by these bodies that many riding schools do not actually refer to themselves as such: in addition to 'riding stables', they may use terms such as 'equestrian centre', 'school of equitation' and '— — — — Riding Ltd.'. In Britain, however, it is extremely unlikely that a riding school will refer to itself as a 'riding club'. This is at variance with countries such as Germany, where many establishments which perform the functions of riding schools call themselves 'clubs' and are legally constituted as such. The term 'riding club' in Britain usually refers to an amateur association of individuals, who come together for competitions and to organise functions such as equestrian outings, lectures and occasional instructional 'clinics' for members. While they may own or lease facilities of some sort, and perhaps be broadly based on a riding school, they do not offer tuition to non-members. They are, however, not usually exclusive, and some (more frequently, the urban-based clubs) have a policy of encouraging novices. Many riders, in due course, join a local riding club and derive considerable pleasure and education from their membership.

It makes no difference to the beginner whether he goes to a large or small riding school for his lessons. It is not the size of the establishment which is important, but the way in which things are run and, as has been stated, the quality of the instruction. The latter can vary greatly. Riding instruction is a bone of contention in the horse world. There are sufficient trainers, but not sufficient good ones.

A former cavalryman may be an excellent trainer, but his training may be nothing more than the meaningless rehearsal of military drills. The riding school owner's eighteen-year-old daughter, who has won a couple of easy jumping competitions, may be an excellent instructress, or she may think her job is just to make sure that no one falls off, and that the ride is always going round in a nice circle.

Highly qualified, instructors may be greatly involved with competition riders, but have no interest in teaching beginners. However, the stout, elderly gentleman whom nobody has ever seen on a horse, and who has no teaching qualification, may be just the person to provide excellent instruction for beginners.

There are few certain indications of a good riding instructor, but one thing is that he must remember that the rider is a customer and must feel that he is really being treated like a customer. He should not be shouted at; this does still happen, though fortunately not very often. After a few lessons it should be possible to judge how good the instructor is by asking yourself whether you understand what he says and what he is trying to put across. For the beginner it is unimportant whether the instructor has won a medal in the Olympics, all that matters is his talent as a teacher. You may find it surprising that many world famous riders are incapable of explaining how you make a horse trot, whereas a young lass who has recently taken her exams may be able to bring on beginners to a high standard in a short time. Many people play tennis, and anyone who has held a tennis racquet in his hand knows how hard it is to always hit the ball correctly. The beginner knows that his early faults will be very difficult to correct later. When a player has become used to holding the racket incorrectly, it takes a long time to learn to hold it correctly. Indeed, he may never succeed. It is the same with riding, and, because it involves another living creature, riding is harder than tennis.

It is therefore a false economy to go for cheap riding lessons if 'cheap' is synonymous with 'bad'. There is nothing wrong with going on an economically priced 'package' course to get some idea as to whether you are going to enjoy this sport or not, but you should avoid going to some really down-market establishment with a couple of long-suffering crocks standing around, and where the owner, instead of instruction, deals out resounding slaps on the horses' rumps. The small amount of money to be saved here is a drop in the ocean. Stables should be as tidy and clean as possible, but stables are a working environment – there are times when it is impossible to have them looking 'clean' from a visitor's point of view. We might also ask if horses can be comfortable in a stable in which you could 'eat off the floor'.

It is difficult for a beginner to judge whether stables are tidy or not. His assessment will often be based on criteria which are of little or no importance. The most important thing is the well-being of the horses; the well-being of the rider is of secondary importance.

A recommendation to a particular stable can also help, but a distinction must be drawn between the recommendation of other beginners, and that of more experienced riders. Beginners can only comment on their impression of the instruction, and what they think they have learned. Not too much notice should be taken of what they say about the way the horses are kept and how the place is run. Observations of this type should only be heeded when they come from experienced riders who are known to have the necessary circumspection, sense of perspective and specialised knowledge.

After a few years' experience of riding and 'horse people', you come to realise how much misinformation is given out of ignorance, and a rider's over-estimation of his own knowledge. A rider who has been riding a couple of times a week for two, three, four, or even five years, still has insufficient knowledge to give a beginner proper advice: the few exceptions only serve to confirm the rule.

Many beginners think that, once they have read a book on the subject, they are ready to take part in the Olympics, but talking about it in the riding club bar is a lot easier than actually going out and doing it.

The First Visit

When visiting a stable for the first time, do not overestimate your riding ability, no-one expects the beginner to have expert knowledge. A little reserve is never a bad thing.

Treat the stables with respect and note the establishment's rules (some stables have rules, others, unfortunately, have none at all). For example, never go into stables with a lighted cigarette in your hand, even though you will keep finding stables where people do smoke. Put out the cigarette, at the latest, outside the door. What you do later in stables where people do smoke (and it is always against the Fire Regulations) is up to you, but smoking should always be taboo.

Many beginners, the first time they go to the riding school, go straight back home without doing what they went for, simply because they do not know whom to go and see when they get there. The chief riding instructor, who in most cases is the person to speak to, is not, of course, waiting at the door or in the office with open arms — he has a lot to do. Since most first visits take place in the evening, he is probably in the middle of the school, giving a lesson. It is, therefore, necessary to wait until the end of the lesson. You can put the time to good use by watching the lesson. It would be presumptuous to think that you will be able to judge the quality of the instruction, but you can watch what happens during a riding lesson, and see whether the instructor is of the loudly-spoken military type, or of a quieter disposition.

You will perhaps feel a bit conspicuous and overdressed if you turn up for this first visit in full riding kit. The riding stable is where people spend their leisure time, and they tend to be dressed accordingly.

When the instructor has finished his lesson, you should let him know you are there. He may have time to talk to you, or he may ask you to wait a bit longer because he has some more instruction or work to do. You should spend the remaining time observing the running of the stables and school. If you are not too shy and diffident, talk to another rider and ask a few questions, or get him to show you where places such as the tackroom are.

Keep your distance from the horses to start with because not only can you never be quite sure how they will react, but also because you are only a visitor. If you go to a garage, you do not jump into every car which is standing around, so do not go into a strange stable, and slap every horse on the rump or dole out lumps of sugar all round; the owners are often not very pleased about the extra calories! Young, horse-mad girls are in the majority at riding stables. They are between ten and twenty-five years of age, and spend all their spare time at the stables.

If you do not have enough time to stand around waiting to speak to the instructor, you should telephone beforehand to book your lesson. The first conversation should be limited to the most important technical details: when is the lesson, what time should you be there, and what should you wear? Although, understandably, you will be feeling unsure of yourself, now is not the time to engage in a discussion on the theory of riding: riding is learnt by riding.

When the booking has been made, the first step has been taken. If you are not in a hurry, there is no harm in having a look round. You should behave like a guest. Do not tear every door open to see what is behind it, and try, as far as possible, not to get in the way of riders and horses. Even friendly questions – 'How old is this chap, then?', 'Isn't he big!' – are rarely well received, and almost always sound fatuous. When you have been going there for a few weeks or months and are part of things, you will realise!

7

Riding Clothes

They must be practical — they may be fashionable

If you learn surfing in the spring or autumn, you must wear thermal clothing, or you will freeze in the cold water, and, even a beginner at the wheel of a racing car will have to wear a fireproof suit from the outset, on safety grounds.

A person starting to ride does not have to look like an Olympic dressage rider. Again and again, we hear riding referred to as a sport for all, but it is still an expensive business, and we should not add unnecessarily to the list of essential items.

Naturally, as a herd animal, man has an urge to conform to his environment as far as possible (in this respect he is like his partner, the horse), but it is quite unnecessary to appear for your first lesson dressed in full riding attire. It is sensible to wait a while, because, who knows if you will carry on with this sport? It may turn out not to be so much fun as you thought at the beginning. Maybe you will not get on with the riding instructor, and, gradually, you may lose interest.

The rider will go through three stages in the way he dresses. The first is the beginner stage, with just a pair of breeches or jodhpurs and a pair of boots or sturdy shoes. Then comes the stage at which his enthusiasm grows, and he dresses himself up to the nines in full riding attire. Finally comes the stage at which he really does begin to have some knowledge, and his sole consideration is that his clothes should be comfortable and practical. Many riders, and you see this at every riding school, get stuck at the second stage.

The beginner should concern himself with only two things: his footwear must be suitable for riding, and he must wear trousers in which he can sit comfortably in the saddle.

If you have about £70 available for this purpose, go to a specialist riding shop and buy a pair of rubber riding boots [£15−£25] and a well-fitting, but sensibly priced, pair of breeches or jodhpurs. Alternatively, many riding schools and even riding shops keep a supply of second-hand items, enabling you to kit yourself out in boots and breeches quite cheaply.

However, even these basic items are not absolutely essential. Nearly everyone has a pair of well-fitting rubber or leather boots at home in the shoe cupboard. Above all, they should be a good fit around the heel. If the boots hang loosely about the foot, the foot position will be affected. You can now also get trainer-type shoes made with a proper heel, which makes them safe for riding. They reach above the ankle, and fit well around the heel, and are, therefore, very suitable for the early lessons. Initially, it is not

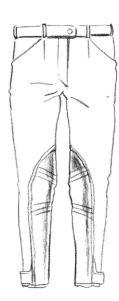

Traditional riding breeches: close-fitting around the calves. The patches inside the knees are either leather, suede or self-stretch material. Breeches end just below the calf and are worn with long boots.

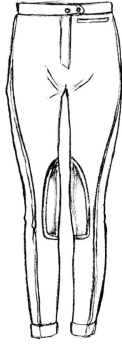

Jodhpurs are longer in the leg than breeches, finishing at the ankle. They have turn-ups, and are traditionally worn with jodhpur boots.

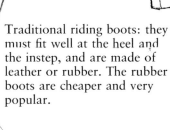

Traditional riding boots: they must fit well at the heel and the instep, and are made of leather or rubber. The rubber boots are cheaper and very popular.

Jodhpur boots: invented by English soldiers in India.

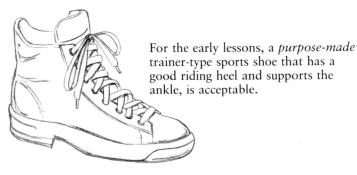

For the early lessons, a *purpose-made* trainer-type sports shoe that has a good riding heel and supports the ankle, is acceptable.

necessary to have boots which reach up to the knee, Experienced riders often prefer them because of the way the leg is used to give the aids, but this can confidently be ignored for the purpose of the early lessons.

If you cannot get hold of a pair of breeches to start with, wear a pair of trousers made of as coarse a material as possible, to stop you sliding about in the sadddle. However, the material should also be fairly soft and comfortable, and should not have folds or creases in it, since these would rub. An old, well-fitting pair of jeans is ideal for the first few lessons. Jackets, jumpers etc., should be comfortable and suitable for the weather conditions, and for safety's sake jewellery should not be worn.

Glasses should fit properly, not be able to move about, and not require adjusting, because this can break a beginner's concentration.

For your own safety, a hard hat is essential, either in the form of the traditional-style riding hat or the skull-cap. Both styles have hard outer shells which protect the head from injury in the case of a bad fall. The chin-strap should always be done up, so that the hat cannot fall off in the event of an accident, which would defeat the object of wearing one. In most stables you are not allowed to ride without a hat. Hats are relatively expensive, so to save extra outlay for your early lessons, ask your instructor before the lesson if it is possible to hire a hat from the riding school.

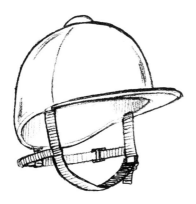

8

The Horse in the Stable

It is unfortunate that, in many riding establishments, the stable is a sort of garage for horses. The horse was not designed by nature to be ridden by man, and then to spend the rest of his time in a 10 m square cage known as a loosebox.

The way a horse is kept depends on what it is used for. Obviously, breeding stock, which may not be ridden much (if at all), is out in the field as much as possible. Riding horses, however, which are ridden for several hours every day, are more conveniently kept in boxes — more conveniently that is from the rider's point of view.

Even in stables, horses form a herd. It would be preferable if they did not have to be separated by walls or bars, and could make physical contact, but in most riding establishments, keeping the horses separate is unavoidable for a variety of reasons. The composition of the horse population is constantly shifting, and horses sometimes change boxes. Horses which have to stand next to each other, have to get used to each other, and a pecking order has to be established. This is not achieved without a lot of screaming, and even kicking and biting, which will, for the first few days, upset the whole equine community.

In many riding schools, the owners come at odd times of the day to give their horses titbits. If there were no partitions between the boxes, there would be a riot every time one horse received a carrot while the others did not.

Fortunately, not many establishments nowadays have stalls. Stalls are compartments in which the horses are tied up and have to stand, unable to move around freely, and are only really acceptable if the horses are ridden or lunged for many hours each day.

The horse feels secure in his box; he knows no safer place anywhere. When he gets frightened, or feels the need to run away, he will always run into his box because it is his home, and he feels instinctively that he will be protected within the stable herd. In the stable the horse is never asked to do anything unfamiliar, and, above all, that is where he is fed.

Horses have relatively small stomachs, and so are fed two or three times per day. In the wild, on the steppes, the horse is constantly moving about, with his nose on the ground, grazing. Even modern horses, if left in the field day and night with plenty of grass, spend about twenty hours per day eating. Only during the hottest part of the day do they stop walking around from one tuft of grass to another.

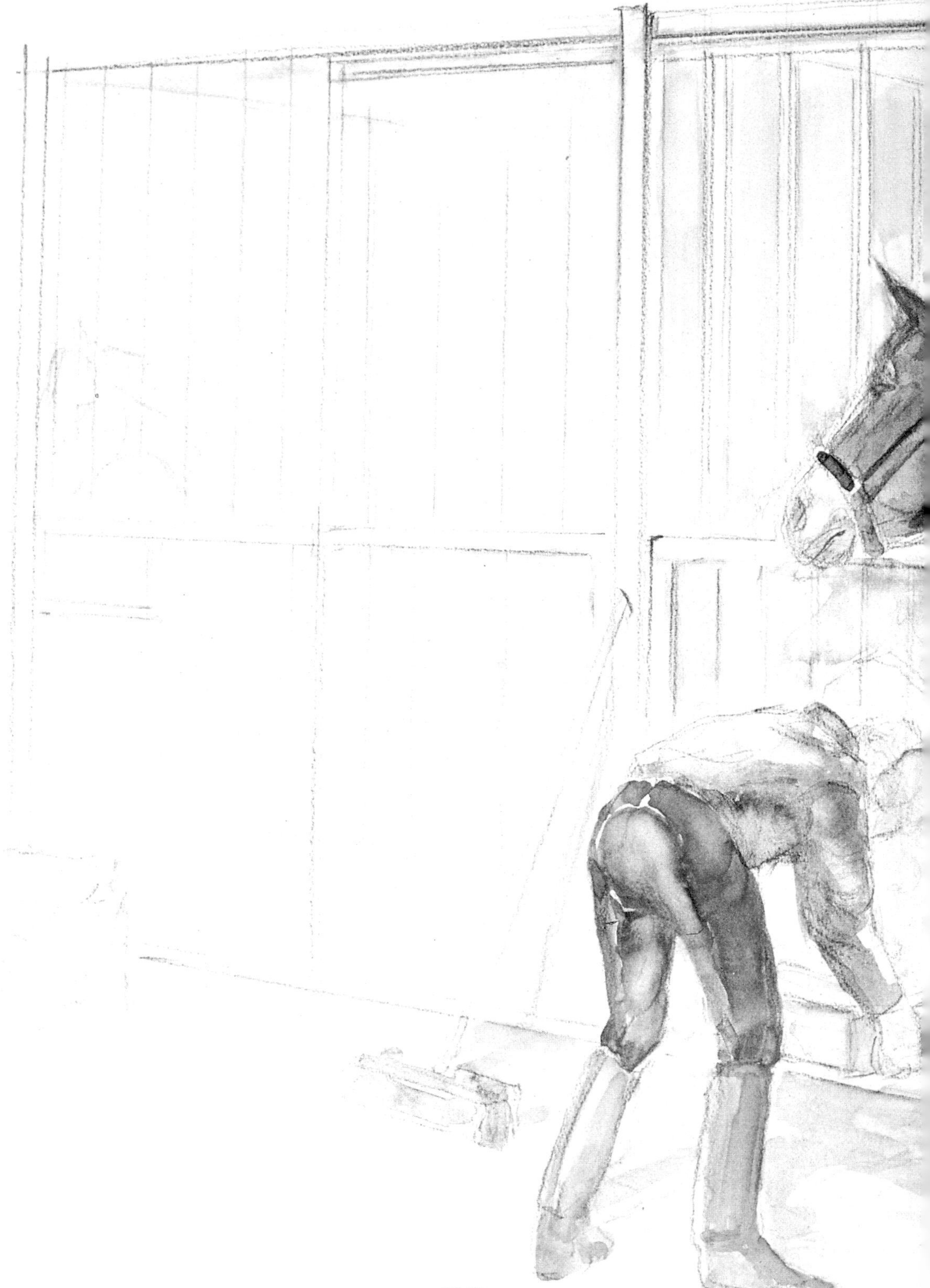

It is for this reason that horses should be fed as frequently as possible. Unlike predatory animals, such as dogs or cats, horses cannot eat large quantities of food all at once, and then go without for a long time. Even when horses are stabled, it is noticeable that most of them have their heads on the floor, eating straw, long after the hay has run out.

When you approach a horse in his box, or stall, you must understand that it is like entering someone else's house; behave like a visitor, and be calm and friendly. Before opening the stable door, speak to the horse to ensure that he has noticed you are there. Many stable doors become slightly misshapen with age, and cannot be opened very easily, so take care to open them without making too much noise to avoid startling the horse. On your first visit, take a small present with you; horses like a titbit by way of introduction, and will walk up to the door wondering what treat is about to appear from your pocket. (I am a great believer in giving titbits, but some stables disapprove of this as a matter of policy, so it is wise to check first.)

Do not go into the box if the horse turns his quarters on you. This may just be his personal foible (horses, like people, behave differently), and when you know this is the case, you can go in as normal because there is no danger. However, it may be that the horse is a kicker, so a novice should not enter the stable without experienced help.

Even if he cannot do so on his first visit, the beginner should spend plenty of time making contact with, and handling, the horse in the box. Rule number one: no sudden movements, do everything quietly and calmly. What, then, is the meaning of 'calm'? Go into the box, offer the titbit, and try to stroke the horse. Even at this point you will be able to see how you should move. If your first movement is too quick, the horse will throw his head up, and perhaps run into the opposite corner of the box. If he is a well-trained school horse, and these are usually of a mature age, he will know that there is no real danger from the sudden movement – he will have seen it all before.

Although no one is taught it any more, in days gone by when horses were still a common form of transport, even townschildren used to learn that titbits should always be offered on the palm of the hand. Most horses will then take them very carefully, with their lips. If you offer the horse a titbit with your fingers alone, you might get one of your fingers bitten. The horse does not do it on purpose, he just cannot distinguish it from the carrot.

Many horses wear a headcollar in the stable. This makes it easier to catch hold of the horse. If you want to pat the horse's neck, hold the head-

collar with one hand, and pat the horse with the other. This prevents the horse jumping back out of fear or surprise the first time you touch him. Holding the headcollar also stops him playfully pulling your jacket, or nipping your arm. Playful nipping should not be encouraged, because although it is not really dangerous (the worst you will get is a bruise), it hurts, so people who are not used to horses tend to let out a yell of surprise, and that in itself can upset or frighten the horse. Therefore, always speak in a quiet, calm tone of voice, as slowly as possible, without yelling or shrieking. The important thing is not what you say to the horse, but the tone in which you say it.

Getting to Know the Horse by Grooming Him

The initial contact with the horse has been made. The thing to do next is really to get to know the horse by grooming him. Every true rider grooms his horse himself. Only if you get to know the individual peculiarities of this living being, can you react appropriately to these peculiarities when you are in the saddle. Moreover, as with people, no two horses are alike. Not only is grooming beneficial to the well-being of the horse's coat and skin, but also the majority of horses find it a pleasurable experience, and this helps cement a bond between horse and rider. In addition, many horses

1) Mane comb
2) Body brush
3) Rubber curry comb
4) Hoof pick with square hole at the end for fitting studs in horse's shoes.
5) Cotton stable rubber
6) Sponge

recognise grooming as a prelude to work.

Some riding schools encourage pupils to groom and tack up the horses; learning these skills is part of the tuition. At other stables, however, you may need to make a special arrangement for these lessons.

Most horses are more than happy to get out of their boring stables at last, and pleased that they are going to be groomed and ridden; it breaks up the monotony of daily life. Some horses, however, are afraid of the work and exertion which nearly always follows the grooming, and prefer to stay in their stables and do nothing. These horses need an encouraging word, or even a slap, to make them leave their boxes.

The tail hairs are individually 'teased' apart. In this way, no hairs are pulled out, and the horse keeps his beautiful, full tail.

The horse should be tied up with a special knot which can quickly be pulled undone if he panics. Insets: left − picking out a hoof, right − quick-release knot.

9

Good Equipment is Good Insurance

Good Equipment is Good Insurance

Saddles and bridles should be kept in a room specially allocated for this purpose. This is called a tack room. As far as possible, this room should be free of dust, dry, and well ventilated. Leather riding equipment is expensive, but the main reason for taking care of it and cleaning and oiling it regularly is that it will otherwise become brittle, and thus become prone to breaking and a danger to rider and horse.

The Headcollar is the Horse's 'Handle'

When an inexperienced rider goes into a tack room, he is confronted with a miscellaneous collection of saddles, bridles and other equipment. Sorting out what is what seems like an art in itself, but it is not as difficult as it seems. Let us start with the simplest piece of equipment, the headcollar, which can be made of leather or nylon.

The headcollar serves a number of purposes. Most importantly, it enables us to hold onto the horse and catch him more easily if he is turned out in a field; it is, in effect, a handle.

Horses are familiarised with the headcollar at an early age. Wearing it should become second nature to them, and even foals, during their first few days of life, are taught to wear one. The headcollar and lead-rope are used to lead the horse out of the stable, to tie him up, and to lead him from place to place.

Before the horse can be led or tied up, the headcollar must be put on correctly. Stand on the left (near) side of the horse's head, undo the buckle or fastening on the left cheekpiece thus releasing the headpiece. Slip the nose-

band over the horse's nose, then pass the headpiece over the horse's head, from the right (off) side, behind the ears, and rebuckle the cheekpiece on the left side. The headcollar should fit loosely and not exert any pressure. It should not, however, be so loose that the horse can rub it off.

Be gentle when handling the ears, many horses are sensitive in this area. This can be one reason why a horse throws his head up when having a head-collar (or bridle) put on. With a horse that has this habit of throwing his head up, pass the right arm under the horse's head and apply a little gentle pressure on his nose with the right hand; this should keep his head down long enough for you to complete the task.

The headcollar, therefore, makes it easier to handle the horse in the stable and in the field. If the horse wears it all the time, frequent checks should be made to ensure that it fits correctly, and that it is not cutting into the skin, or rubbing. Leather headcollars need to be treated frequently with saddle soap and leather dressing to keep them clean, and to ensure, above all, that they do not become hard.

At the back of the headcollar nose-band is a metal ring which, if the head-collar is fitted correctly, lies underneath the jaw. It is to this that the leadrope is attached. This rope can have a quick-release or 'panic' clip at the end, which can be released immediately by the handler if, while the horse is tied up, he

If you need to tie the horse up with something around his neck, while you put the bridle on for example, the headcollar can be used temporarily as a neck strap.

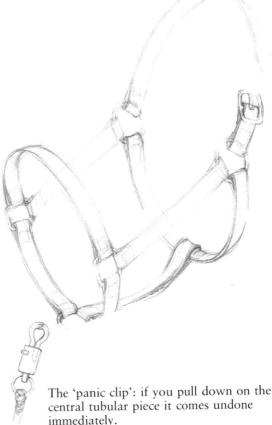

The 'panic clip': if you pull down on the central tubular piece it comes undone immediately.

[41]

pulls back sharply in panic, or if some unforeseen danger arises. Horses calm down very quickly once they are no longer tied up. A quick downward squeeze on the spring-loaded barrel of the clip releases it. Alternatively, leadropes without a quick-release facility should be passed through a loop of baling twine, or breakable string, which is attached to the object to which the horse is to be secured. If the horse pulls back, the twine breaks and neither horse, headcollar nor leadrope are damaged. The rope should also always be tied in a quick-release knot.

Horses tied up in stalls sometimes wear a neckstrap instead of a headcollar. A headcollar can be used as a neckstrap quite easily. This is particularly useful if you are out hacking (riding in the country) and need to take a headcollar with you to tie the horse up when you stop. A horse must not be tied up by the bridle. It is also a good idea to use the headcollar as a neckstrap in the case of horses which cannot wear a proper headcollar for a while owing to sore places or wounds of some kind.

Bridle with snaffle bit and drop noseband.

The Bridle

The term 'bridle' describes the leatherwork which holds the bit in the horse's mouth, and encompasses the reins and the bit itself.

The essential element of the bridle for controlling the horse is the applied action of the bit, and this may be supplemented by the action of certain types

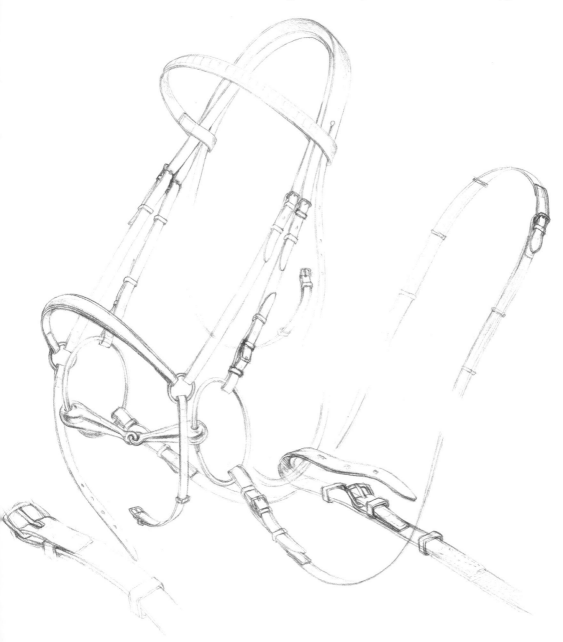

Bridle with jointed snaffle bit and drop noseband unbuckled prior to fitting, plus detail of how reins buckle to bit ring.

[43]

of noseband. There are various types of bit, the most common being the snaffle. This, in turn, has numerous designs, but is typified by providing a direct link between the rein action and the horse's mouth, whereas other types of bit also incorporate some degree of leverage on the horse's lower jaw. The snaffle is by far the most suitable bit for novice riders, being the easiest to use correctly, and mild in action when so used.

The noseband, as the name suggests, is the part of the bridle that fits round the horse's nose between his cheeks and his nostrils. The precise location is dictated by the type of noseband and this is determined by the required function. The nosebands most commonly used for ordinary riding are the 'cavesson', 'drop' and 'flash'.

The cavesson simply fits around the horse's nose about halfway between his cheekbones and the corners of his mouth. It has no influence on the action of the bit and, indeed, its function is largely decorative, except when it is used in conjunction with a 'standing martingale', which we shall discuss shortly. The drop noseband fits considerably lower down than the cavesson, and fastens around the horse's mouth just below the bit. Correctly

Bridle with snaffle bit and flash noseband.

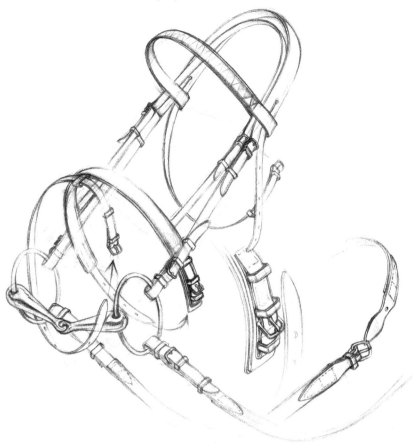

Bridle with jointed snaffle bit and flash noseband unbuckled prior to fitting, plus detail of the cavesson noseband fastening, and the rein fastening.

adjusted (as it must be), it transfers a little of the rein effect onto the horse's nasal bone, but its main purpose is to prevent the horse from opening his mouth wide or 'crossing his jaw' – evasions which would make him harder to control. However, the drop noseband has long been popular in Britain and almost standard equipment in various other countries, so its presence does not necessarily indicate that the wearer has proved problematical in these areas.

The flash noseband is a kind of cross between a cavesson and a drop. It consists, in effect, of a cavesson with an additional strap. This strap fits through a loop in the front of the cavesson and passes down and around the horse's mouth, acting in much the same way as a drop. The advantages of the flash are that the second strap can be employed or dispensed with as required, and it is less likely to interfere with a horse's breathing than a poorly-adjusted drop. The flash is gaining in popularity, and may well supercede the drop before long. Once again, its presence does not necessarily indicate difficulties in the horse.

Other types of bridle which might be noticed in the tackroom, but which a novice should not be expected to use, include those with a 'grackle' noseband, double bridles, and hackamores.

The grackle consists of two leather straps crossing each other on the horse's nose, one passing above, and one below, the bit. Fitted, it looks similar to a flash, but it cannot be converted to a cavesson. While it performs functions similar to a flash, it is also designed to transfer some rein effect to the horse's nasal bone. It was invented to help control a powerful racehorse, and is often associated with strong, hard-pulling competition horses.

The double bridle has two bits, each operated by a different set of reins, invariably used in conjunction with a simple cavesson noseband. Its purpose is to obtain precise effects in advanced schooling, and it is therefore a bridle for experienced riders on well-trained horses.

The hackamore is a bitless bridle designed to operate by pressure on the horse's nose. It is sometimes used on horses with various mouth problems, but is not suitable for novice riders.

There are other sorts of bridle, but these are specific to different styles of riding, such as Western, and will not be encountered unless a rider explores such styles at a later stage of his career.

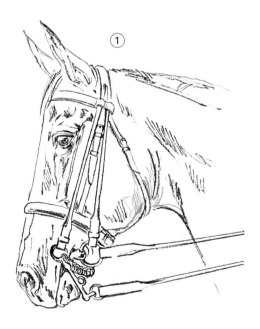

1) The double bridle with cavesson noseband, bridoon (a small-ringed snaffle with a thin mouthpiece) and a long-cheeked curb bit with curb chain. The double bridle has two sets of reins; one attached to the snaffle bit and the other set attached to the curb bit.

2) The hackamore, or bitless bridle, operates by pressure on the horse's nose.

Bandages and Boots

To protect their legs, and also to support tendons and ligaments, horses often wear bandages or 'boots' on the fore and hind legs.

For competitions, horses wear bandages (coloured bandages are very popular), but these often fulfil only a cosmetic function. For training and horse trials, boots are fitted, to protect the legs from knocks. When ridden across country, the horse can easily knock himself against a branch or a large stone, but injury can also be self-inflicted by one or other of his hooves striking another leg.

Boots are relatively easy to put on, but novices should not use bandages without expert guidance. Bandages consist of long strips of strong fabric, and must be put on flat and with even pressure, otherwise they can cause pressure injuries. They are always put on starting at the top (just below the knee), and overlapped slightly. They are secured with velcro, or sewn on. Tapes, tied with knots, should be avoided. The knots can come undone, or, worse, they can cause pressure injuries. As an extra precaution, boots can be put on over bandages for training.

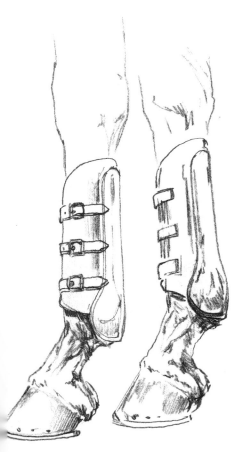

A protective boot and a bandage.

Martingales and Auxiliary Reins

Martingales are leather straps intended to prevent a horse from throwing his head up beyond the point of control, and perhaps hitting his rider in the face. Some riders fit them to young horses who have not established a quiet head carriage, and others to horses who tend to become excitable when jumping. Martingales are sometimes perceived to have other uses but, when applied according to these perceptions, they are usually incorrectly fitted and simply create further problems. There are two types of martingale in common use: 'running' and 'standing'.

A running martingale consists of a neckstrap, which is passed over the horse's head to rest around the base of his neck, and a second strap which is joined to the neckstrap at right angles. One end of this second strap has a loop, and this end is passed between the horse's forelegs, the girth being run through the loop before being fastened. The other end divides into two, each ending in a ring. The left and right reins are each passed through the appropriate ring and refastened, rubber stops being placed on the reins to prevent the rings from sliding down near the horse's mouth.

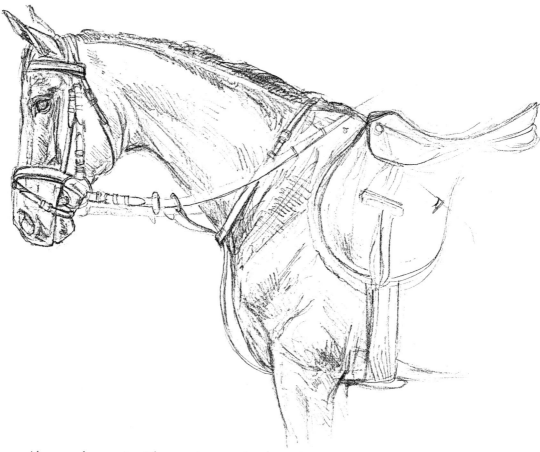

Above and opposite: The running martingale.

The length of the martingale must be adjusted individually for each horse: it must not be so long that it cannot fulfil its function but, if it is too short, it will interfere with the rein aids, increasing the pressure on the horse's mouth *provoking* in him the very resistances it is intended to alleviate. A general guide to correct adjustment is that, if the ring end of a martingale is held up vertically by hand, it should be level with the horse's wither. If it comes below this, the martingale is definitely too tight.

Some instructors fit running martingales as standard to horses being ridden by beginners, but suitable horses should not normally need them. Conceivably, however, they may be of value to pupils having their first experience of riding in the open, since they may assist in retaining control should the horses become a little excited at being out, and perhaps jumping small obstacles, in company.

A standing martingale is designed much like a running martingale, except that, instead of dividing into two ringed ends, the upper strap has a single, looped, end. This reaches up to the cavesson noseband, which fastens through it. It has no connection to the reins and, whereas the running martingale makes it harder for a horse to raise his head high, the standing martingale makes it impossible.

Although it is a physical preventative, the standing martingale has no remedial effect on a horse, and, indeed, if a horse constantly resists it, he will merely strengthen the muscles underneath his neck and be *more* inclined to carry his head high when the device is removed. For this reason, it is essential that it is not fitted too tightly; a guideline to correct fitting is that, pushed up by hand, there should be just sufficient length for the fitted strap to reach into the horse's gullet. If a horse 'needs' a standing martingale, this probably indicates deficiences in conformation or training beyond simply carrying his head high, and such deficiences would render him an unsuitable ride for a novice.

Besides martingales, there are

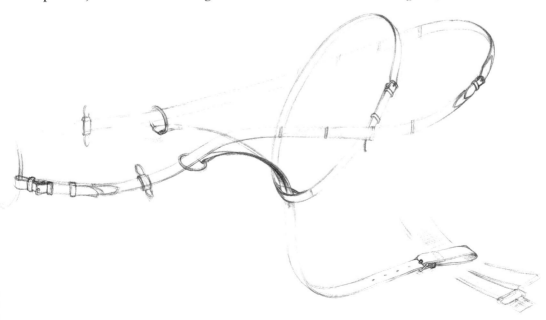

various auxiliary reins intended to assist the rider in improving the horse's acceptance of the aids. Some of these may be of occasional value in the hands of skilled riders when training or reschooling difficult horses, but they should not be used by novices, or as a substitute for skill.

The only auxiliary reins which might be legitimately used to assist a novice rider are 'side reins'. These are leather straps, often with rubber rings inserted to provide some flexibility, and they are used in pairs, one each side of the horse. One end of each side rein attaches to a bit ring, and the other end to the girth on the same side. They should be adjusted so that, when they are just taut, the horse's face is a few degrees in front of the vertical. They should not be used for protracted periods and, at the end of a period of use, they should be removed to allow the horse to stretch his neck.

Side reins are most commonly used when a horse is being lunged (in which case, if he is not saddled, they are attached to a strap called a roller). Although an experienced person has considerable control of a horse when lungeing, this will not be so great as if he were riding, so he may employ side reins to help maintain the horse's outline. Since he may do this in the context of using the horse to give a lunge lesson, a novice rider might become acquainted with side reins if he is introduced to riding in this way.

However, just as side reins may be used to assist an experienced person who is remote from the horse, so they may also be used to assist a rider who is inexperienced in exercising control. This system is frequently employed in Germany, the idea being to give novices the feel of riding a horse who is moving in a correct outline without their having, themselves, to do all that is necessary to attain it.

Many riding schools provide a neck-strap for novice riders. This is simply a leather strap buckled loosely round the base of the horse's neck. Its purpose being to provide something for the rider to hold onto should he feel insecure.

10

The Saddle

'Saddle' is a word which has given rise to various associated expressions. You become 'firm in the saddle', you 'saddle up', or you can 'ride in all saddles'.

Not only is the saddle the most expensive item of tack, but it is also an extremely important and essential piece of equipment.

For general purpose riding we use a basic form of saddle, and variations of this are used for the specialised disciplines. Other styles of riding, naturally, require saddles of a different design. The Western rider uses a Western saddle, and the vaquero (a mounted Spanish herdsman) uses his own special kind of saddle. The riding styles of mounted stockmen (cowboys, vaqueros, gauchos) can be classified as working styles. For these styles, there are only two criteria for judging the style of horsemanship and, of course, the equipment used: they must serve their purpose as far as possible, and they must be as comfortable as possible.

The classical art of equitation originated in the battlefield and later developed as a refined form of riding, the aim of which was the pure enjoyment of riding, and to make the horse perform beautiful, elevated paces. It was an end in itself, and the pleasure was derived from the harmony of the movements.

Since riding nowadays is mostly an end in itself, either as a leisure activity or a sport, this classical style is taught in just about all the riding schools in Europe, and far beyond, although other forms, such as Western riding are also taught.

The saddle you use for your first lesson is usually a general purpose saddle. Its name refers to its suitability for use for either dressage, jumping or cross-country riding. There are also two specialised saddles which are slightly different from each other; the jumping saddle and the dressage saddle.

The jumping rider needs a saddle which will give him as much support as possible, and allows him to keep his legs in the jumping position. The jumping saddle has a more pronounced dip in the seat, and underneath the flaps, has knee-rolls in front of his leg, and thigh-rolls behind his leg. The purpose of these rolls, or pads, is to stop the leg sliding too far forward or too far back.

The dressage rider sits considerably deeper into the horse than the jumping rider. His saddle has very long flaps, with no padding under the rider's leg, so that the latter can lie flat against the horse.

It takes a long time for the novice to reach the stage where he can specialise, and so need a special saddle.

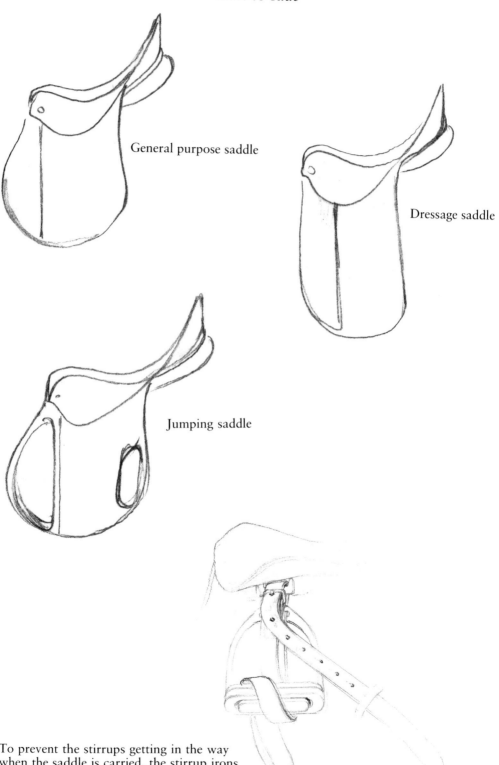

General purpose saddle

Dressage saddle

Jumping saddle

To prevent the stirrups getting in the way
when the saddle is carried, the stirrup irons
are run up the leathers and secured like this.

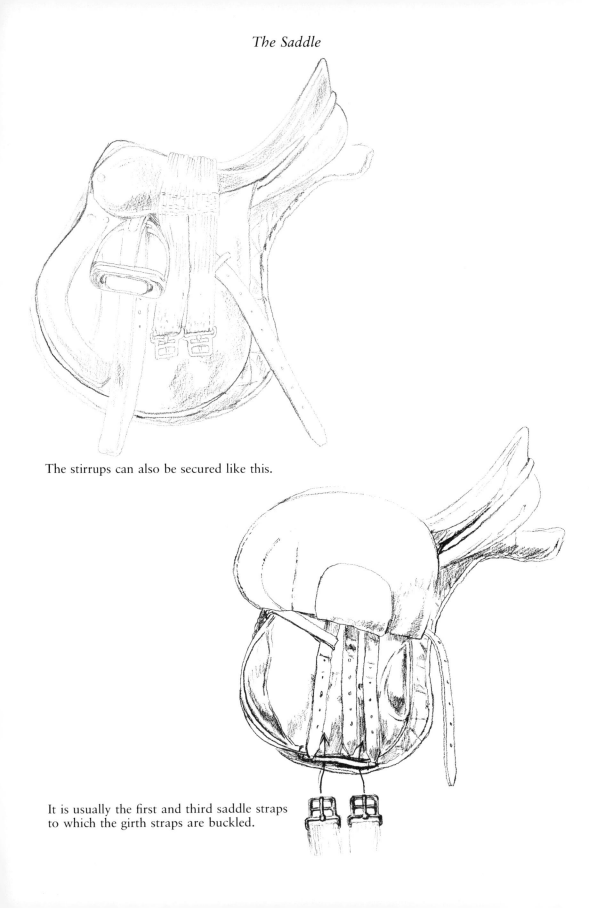

The stirrups can also be secured like this.

It is usually the first and third saddle straps to which the girth straps are buckled.

11
Before You Ride, You Must Saddle Up

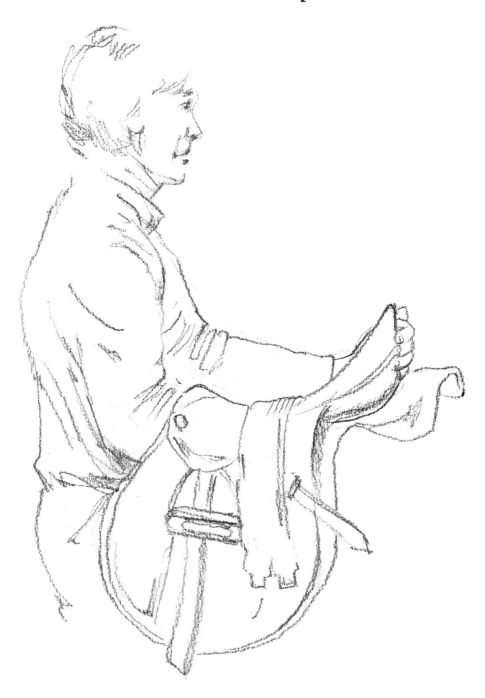

Everyone is excited before his first riding lesson. It is quite normal for the heart to beat faster, and, some people have a job to control their nerves. Thousands of beginner riders have experienced these feelings — so why should you be any different? It is the same nervousness you experience on your first encounter with a horse, or the first time you groom one.

12

If the Saddle Does Not Sit Right,
Neither Will the Rider

At first it seems almost impossible to get the bridle over the horse's head. Everyone is confused initially by all the different straps, and nervousness of the horse's great big mouth with its yellow teeth makes it difficult to get the bit in! Then up goes the head out of reach! Putting the saddle on seems a lot easier: just slap it on and yank it tight!

In fact, putting the saddle on correctly and gently is of vital importance; it must be positioned at exactly the right spot. It is placed well forward,

on the withers, and then slid back — always in the direction of the lie of the hair — until it is in the right place.

At this point, the stirrups are at the top of the leathers, and the girth is lying across the seat of the saddle. Not until the saddle is in the correct position is the girth taken off the top. However, before it is done up, you must check that the numnah (saddle pad) is lying flat all round, and has not slipped or become creased. The saddle should never be put on without a numnah. It relieves the pressure of the leather on the horse's back, and absorbs the sweat, considerable amounts of which build up quickly under the saddle. When the numnah has been straightened, the girth (which is already buckled to the saddle on the right hand side) is passed under the horse's stomach, and fastened on the left side of the saddle. At least three straps are provided on the saddle for this purpose, but there are only two buckles on the girth. The reason for this is safety. The front two saddle straps are on one piece of webbing, the third is on a separate piece of web. So, providing the girth straps are fastened to the first and third, or second and third saddle straps, should one of the straps break, the other strap will hold the girth in place until the problem is rectified.

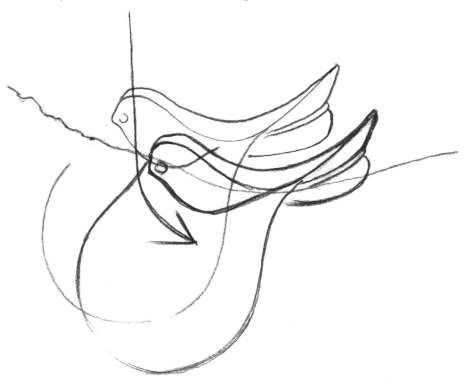

The saddle is placed well forward on the withers, and then slid back (to ensure the hair lies correctly) into place.

It is worth mentioning that, when handling a horse, all the important things are done on the left hand side: horses are led from the left, saddled from the left, straps are buckled on the left, and riders mount from the left and dismount to the left. The reason behind this is simple. The old mounted warriors carried their sabres on the right, and, later, the cavalrymen carried their pistols on the same side. They had to mount on the left so that the sabre or holster did not get in the way. The right hand was kept free for fighting and shooting. Nowadays, doing everything from the left no longer has any practical value, but is, nevertheless, still practised.

The girth must be tight, not only because if it is left loose the saddle will slip sideways when you mount — which gives everyone a good laugh — but also because a loose fitting saddle rubs the horse's back, which can result in nasty pressure injuries; these are popularly known as saddle sores. They are only small, but because they are in an important position, a horse can be out of action for many weeks. When the girth is fastened, there should be a hand's breadth between the girth and the horse's elbow. When you have put the saddle on and done up the girth, ask your instructor, or an experienced rider, to check that the position is correct.

When the girth is fastened there should be a hand's breadth between the girth and the horse's elbow.

13

Putting On the Bridle is Not as Difficult as it Seems

Putting on the bridle is a bit more complicated than putting on the saddle, but when you have done it a couple of times you will be surprised at how quickly you get the hang of it and how easy it becomes.

Stand on the left of the horse, facing in the same direction. Pass the reins over the horse's head and onto the neck. You can then take off the headcollar, because the horse can be held by the reins around its neck, like a neckstrap, if necessary. The right hand holds the headpiece of the bridle and the left hand holds the bit. The right hand supports the whole bridle in front of the horse's head. Then the left hand gently pushes the bit into the horse's mouth, while the right hand lifts the bridle which is then eased over the ears.

Some horses do not open their mouths immediately. However, when the metal bit is in contact with their lips, they will open their mouths if slight pressure is applied, and the bit can be pushed in. With some horses, you may have to press your left thumb gently on the gum, behind the incisor teeth, to get them to open their mouths. The horse has no teeth in this part of the jaw (you should look beforehand!). The incisors are at the front of the jaw, behind which are sometimes to be found single pointed teeth known as wolf teeth (top jaw) and tushes (lower jaw), then there is a section about ten centimetres long without any teeth. Behind this are the premolars and the molars. In horsey language, the sections with no teeth are known as the 'bars' of the mouth which is where the bit lies. The bit acts on the lower jaw and the tongue. You should make sure that the bit is actually on top of the tongue, and not underneath it. At first, your riding instructor will check this, but later, you will be able to do so yourself.

Buckle the throatlatch and the noseband. The throatlatch goes round the throat and behind the horse's ears, and is fastened very loosely on the left (there should be at least a fist's breadth between it and the throat).

The cavesson noseband is fastened inside the cheekpieces and above the bit, with two fingers' width between the noseband and the horse's face to allow flexion of the jaw. The dropped noseband is fastened below the bit, and should be buckled tighter than the cavesson — as a general rule you should be able to fit a thumb between it and the horse's nose — but if it is done up too tightly, it interferes with the horse's breathing.

Before fastening the bridle straps, the rider must check that the bridle fits correctly, that no straps are twisted, and that the forelock is outside the browband. Horses' heads are extremely sensitive, so care should always be taken, especially around the ears.

Supporting the bridle
with the right hand
ready to lift it when the
left hand has placed the
bit in the horse's
mouth. In this position,
the right hand can also
apply a little pressure
to the horse's nose to
keep his head down if
he tends to throw it up.

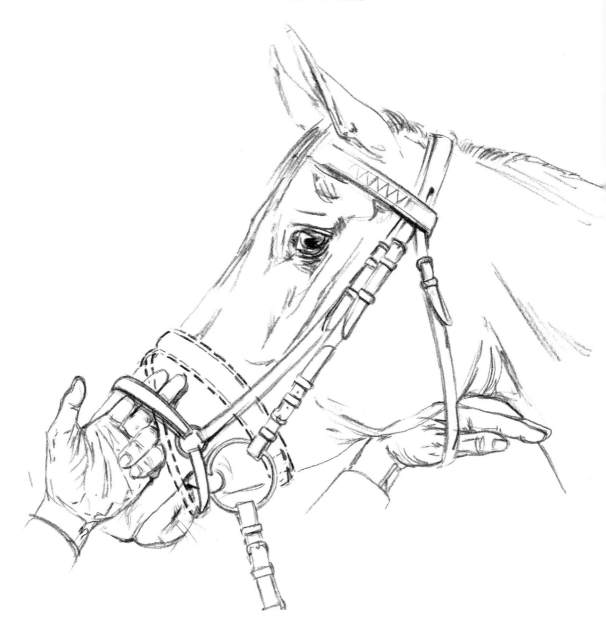

The correct fitting of the bridle showing the room required.

14

Into the School

The horse is bridled and saddled, so what comes next? First the horse must get from the stable to the place where the first lesson is going to take place. Is he supposed to find his own way there? Of course not – he can think of better ways to spend twenty minutes or half an hour than going round in circles just so that you can learn to ride!

The horse must be led to the indoor school or outdoor arena. If you are serious about learning to ride properly, and do not just want to be a 'Sunday afternoon rider', you should make it your job to lead the horse yourself from the outset. Insist on doing so, even if your instructor tries to take the horse. Lead the horse from the left;

leave the reins on the neck, and hold them both together behind the bit with the forefinger inserted between the reins. The horse will walk along next to you. You can also take the reins over the horse's head, and hold them both together, with the right hand, under the horse's chin. The left hand holds the free end of the reins, so that the horse does not tread on them.

'Bring the horses in', says the instructor; the signal for the start of the lesson. This is not always so easy as it sounds, though, actually, there are only two mistakes that you can make: you can be either too timid or too enthusiastic. Either the horse fails to notice that you want to move off,

Leading the horse.

[63]

Tightening the girth from the ground.

or you nearly yank the bridle off over his ears. It is better not to use the reins at all to encourage the horse to move off, but simply, with the reins held loosely in the right hand, take a step forward and encourage the horse by saying 'Walk on', and he should march straight into the school. However, things do not always go according to the rule book. A gentle tug on the reins will wake up a dull school horse, and if still more encouragement is needed, one of the other riders can give the horse a gentle tap from behind.

It is correct to walk next to the horse, on the left, level with his shoulder. In practice, however, you may find yourself level with his head. If the horse tries to slow down and stop, do not yank at the reins, talk to him. Words spoken in a calm, low-pitched voice have a soothing effect, whereas if you speak more sharply and loudly, it livens the horse up.

You also find horses who want to go faster than you do. All you have to do then is resist gently on the reins. You should, however, avoid a pulling match. Once the horse has set his lower jaw against the bit, with your puny strength you will have no chance! Give and take: you will often hear this when you are riding, and this is the way to solve this problem. Let the horse come up against the bit, then immediately yield. You may have to repeat this several times. If, in spite of this, the horse does not calm down, do not let him charge forward. Instead, make him circle round you — several times if necessary. Make sure that the reins do not become twisted or tangled.

Before you get on, the girth should be

pulled up further — known in horsey circles as 'tightening the girth'. After the horse starts to move about, the girth becomes looser, and you will be able to tighten it by at least one hole. This can be done from the ground, or, very easily, from the saddle. In the latter case, someone should hold your horse for you to start with, though later you will be able to dispense with this help.

Next the stirrups are pulled down. There are several different ways of securing the stirrups at the top of the leathers. You must watch, and get someone to show you how to do it, then you will have no problem. Not everything to do with riding is a mystery! You should adjust the length of the stirrup leathers approximately at first, before mounting. As an approximate guide, the stirrups (leathers plus irons) should be about the same length as the rider's arm. Once you are in the saddle, your instructor will help you decide the exact length.

As an approximate guide, the stirrups and leathers should be about the same length as the rider's arm.

15

Into the Saddle

Whenever a beginner has to get on a horse he complains that it is too big! Horses *are* big, and no one should be embarrassed by the fact that his joints do not bend as well as they used to — nearly everyone has the same problem. So do not mention the horse's height, just listen when your instructor is explaining how to mount. Ten centimetres' variation in the height of the horse does not make a fall easier or worse.

To mount, the rider stands on the left facing the rear of the horse, with his left shoulder next to the horse's shoulder. A well-trained horse should stand quietly in the school while the rider mounts, but not every horse will do so, so for the first few times, the horse will probably be held for you, and you will not have to bother about

controlling him with the reins. It is, however, a good thing to practise mounting as if you were on your own, so, with the left hand, hold the reins on the horse's withers just short enough to prevent him moving forward.

Next, the right hand turns the stirrup through 180 degrees, so that when you sit down in the saddle, with your foot exactly parallel to the horse's side, the leather is not twisted. Then place the left foot in the stirrup (with the toe pointing towards the hindquarters), put the left hand, holding the reins, on the front of the saddle (or in the loop sometimes provided on the front of the saddle for this purpose), place the right hand on the back of the saddle (or the right side of the saddle), spring smartly up, pass your right leg over the horse's back, and let it slide down the horse's side until it comes in contact with the stirrup. Take care not to stick your toe into the horse as you swing round, never crash down into the saddle, and do keep concentrating until you are finally seated. A good rider slides softly into the saddle, and does not fall onto the horse's loins.

On at last! First of all you should get used to this new feeling. It looks a long way down, but you soon get over this, and after a few lessons you will no longer take any notice of the height. Those of a nervous disposition may find it some consolation that they are no longer in range of the horse's teeth or hooves!

Mounting: face the rear of the horse and turn the stirrup 180 degrees (so that it is straight when you are in the saddle). (Opposite) Place the left foot in the stirrup, hold the back or offside of the saddle with the right hand and spring into the saddle, landing gently.

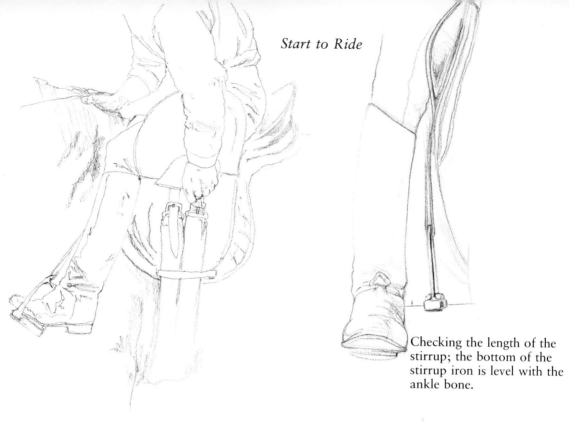

Checking the length of the stirrup; the bottom of the stirrup iron is level with the ankle bone.

Tightening the girth from the saddle.

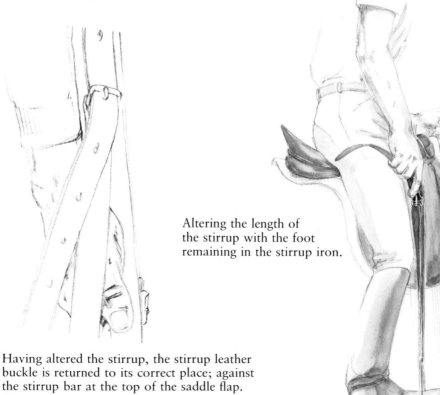

Altering the length of the stirrup with the foot remaining in the stirrup iron.

Having altered the stirrup, the stirrup leather buckle is returned to its correct place; against the stirrup bar at the top of the saddle flap.

[72]

16

Lungeing and Lunge Lessons

'Lunge' comes from the French word *longe*. A lunge rein is actually nothing more than a sort of long rope, on the end of which the horse goes in circles around the trainer (lunger). The diameter of this circle should be between 12 and 14 metres. If it is less than this, excessive weight is placed on the horse's inside legs, and damage can result.

Lungeing gives the lunger control of the horse whether or not there is a rider on board.

The lunge rein is attached to a lungeing cavesson. This is a strengthened form of headcollar with a padded noseband that has three metal rings in it; one in the centre and one at each side. The horse is usually lunged from the centre ring. Occasionally a horse is lunged from the bridle. In this case the lunge rein must go through the inside bit ring (the bit ring nearest the lunger), pass over the horse's head behind the ears and clip to the outside bit ring. With this method the lunge rein has to be changed over when the horse is worked in the opposite direction.

For a beginner's lesson, the horse is often fitted with side-reins which ensure the horse remains in the correct position, or outline, without the rider having to do anything. Side-reins also reduce the risk of high-spirited bucks and resistances. The reins are taken away from the rider and crossed over the horse's neck, so that they do not get in the way, and so that the rider cannot interfere with the horse by, for example, pulling on the reins. First of all, the rider must get the feel of riding at the walk, and it will not hurt to do a few exercises to start with, to improve the balance. If a rider feels insecure he can hold on to the front of the saddle, or the neckstrap, with one hand.

The aim of these early lunge lessons is to give the rider the beginnings of a feel for the correct balance. Then, still without reins, he will learn the rising trot which was developed about one hundred and fifty years ago, as a way to make the trot more comfortable. The rising trot is less strenuous than the sitting trot for both horse and rider, and can be kept up for long distances.

Young horses are worked on the lunge as a preparation for being ridden. Older horses are lunged for the purpose of teaching people to ride. However, no one should feel like a skier on the nursery slopes when he is being lunged. Even Olympic champions continue to ride on the lunge, because it is the only way of testing whether the seat is independent of the reins (and hands).

Lungeing the novice rider.

17

The Walk

The horse has three basic gaits: the walk, the trot and the canter. There are a few breeds of horse which have extra gaits; gaits such as the tölt and the pace. The beginner should ignore these specialised gaits and concentrate on the basic ones.

The walk is a four-time (or four-beat) gait, and has four variations, or speeds: the collected walk (slow and elevated), the working (or 'free') walk, the medium walk, and the extended walk. The trot and canter also have these variations.

In dressage riding, the walk is the most difficult gait which some novices find hard to understand. In walk it is almost impossible to fall off, and the rider does not slide further and further out of the saddle. Yet the walk is a gait without spring. It is difficult, in walk, to create enough action, and so to obtain the required engagement and carriage. A beginner will not necessarily notice this problem, but it becomes obvious to every rider eventually.

Unlike the trot, the walk has little influence on the horse's training. The trot can be considerably improved through correct training, so that a horse which has, by nature, a mediocre trot, learns to give more, that is, to take bigger steps in the trot. Nature does, however, place a limit on the amount of ground a horse can cover in walk. Some horses have a good walk, but others, unfortunately, have less talent for this gait. For the working (free) walk to be correct the hind feet should tread approximately in the prints of the forefeet.

The walk.

The horse stands correctly, on all four legs, on the bit.

The rider braces the back muscles, sits even deeper (heavier) in the saddle, and places the lower legs against the horse's sides (a short distance behind the girth).

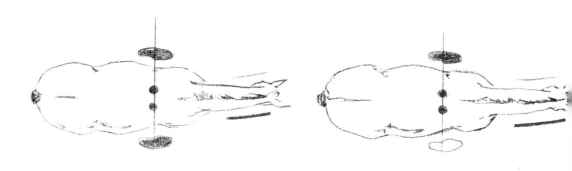

Diagram of the horse in walk, seen from above:
On the outside of the horse are the rider's legs (shaded = driving leg); the two dots are the rider's seat bones (heavier shading = more weight placed on them). The reins are shown along the sides of the neck (thicker line = stronger contact).

The rider now sits straight (or even leans backwards slightly), the horse brings the other foot forward, the hands yield, the legs push, one side at a time — first right, then left, etc.

Every single step must be ridden. The back muscles are still taut, the legs touch the horse alternately, and there is a sensitive contact with the horse's mouth.

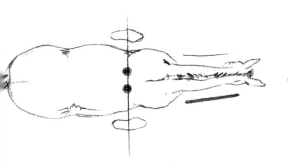

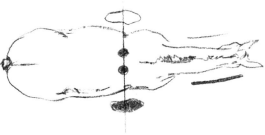

18

The Trot

The trot is a two-time gait. The horse brings the legs forward relatively fast, in diagonal pairs, and sets them down. Imagine a horse standing still, with his weight evenly distributed on all four legs. If he then goes forward into trot, he moves his left foreleg and his right hind leg forward simultaneously. He then does the same with the right foreleg and the left hind leg, and so on. Of course, he may, instead, start off with the right foreleg. Many animals perform a gait called the pace. This is essentially a two-time gait, but it differs from the diagonal trot of the horse in that the two legs on one side move forward together. Elephants pace, and so do camels. Also, as has already been mentioned, there are breeds of horses which can pace as well as trot. Pacing is an undesirable trait in our riding horses, and in dressage it is considered a fault.

The trot is the most important gait for every horse. In the wild, when the horse is moving around in search of food, it is the gait most commonly used, apart from walk. The trot is considerably less strenuous for the horse than the canter. For the novice rider too, the trot is the most important gait. There are two ways to ride in trot: the rising trot which is learned first, because it is easier for beginners, and less strenuous, and the sitting trot when the rider does not rise out of the saddle.

The trot.

The horse is in walk. A half halt is used to prepare him for trot.

There is simultaneous pressure of both legs against the horse, the back muscles are braced, and the rider leans back slightly and sits deep into the saddle.

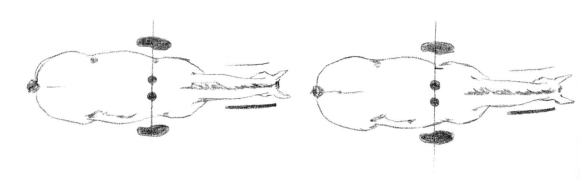

Diagram of the horse in trot, seen from above:
On the outside of the horse are the rider's legs (shaded = driving leg); the two dots are the rider's seat bones (shaded = weight on the seat bones). The reins are shown along the sides of the neck (thicker line = stronger contact).

The horse takes the first step of trot, the hands yield, and the driving aids are increased slightly.

The intensive driving aids increase the action, the horse takes ground-covering strides.

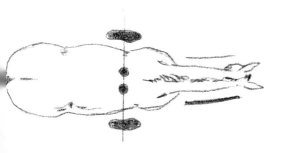 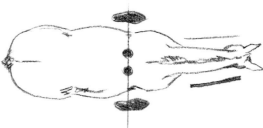

19

The Canter

The canter is a fast gait, although in classical dressage we have the collected canter, which is very elevated and, in the layman's language, slow. Horses in the wild canter (or gallop, which is a faster four-time gait) when they want to get somewhere quickly, or when they are excited and fleeing from imminent danger.

The canter is a three-time gait. It is in this gait that the horse has the greatest difficulty in finding and keeping his balance. The canter is a lateral-orientated gait, so that we have right canter and left canter. In the left canter, when the horse 'leads' with his left foreleg, the sequence is: right hind; left hind and right fore together, and then the left fore. There are three beats in all.

Instruction in canter follows that in walk and trot. On a good school horse, canter is no more difficult to learn than trot. Once you are over the teething troubles, you will find this gait very pleasant and comfortable to ride.

The canter.

The horse is to strike off into canter from trot; the preparation for this is a half halt.

The canter aids are one-sided, so the horse must be flexed to the inside – this is achieved with the inside rein (see arrow on diagram below).

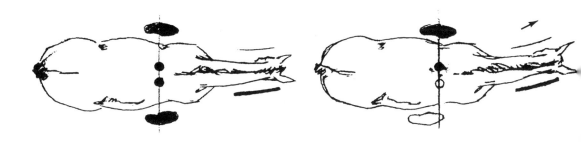

Diagram of the horse in canter, seen from above:
On the outside of the horse are the rider's legs (shaded = driving leg); the two dots are the rider's seat bones (shaded = more weight placed on them). The reins are shown along the sides of the neck (thicker line = stronger contact).

The rider sits on the inside seat bone, the weight is placed on the inside foot, and the inside leg and heel are laid on the horse's side just behind the girth. The outside leg lies further back, in a 'guarding', or 'supporting', position.

The horse canters. The aids (leg, and driving seat) continue to be applied, and must 'trigger' each new canter stride.

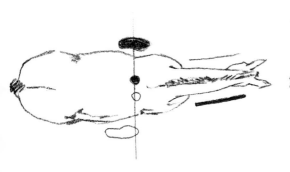

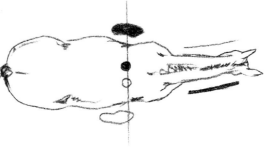

20

The Seat is the Foundation

Riding is difficult at the beginning because all the aids have to be given at once and given correctly. Basically, the rider has to do four or five things simultaneously, and a novice has trouble concentrating on, and coordinating, everything – seat, legs, reins etc. An experienced rider no longer thinks about it. He can give the necessary aids instinctively because they have become second nature. Giving the aids is much easier if the rider is in the correct position in the saddle.

Having said that all the aids should be given simultaneously, it is easier for the beginner to understand if each subject is taken separately, so we will start with the seat.

The correct seat, and the one to strive for, is called the independent seat. This expression will not mean much to the beginner, and needs to be explained. The rider should be supple and free from tension. His knees should not be clamped against the saddle, he should not be holding on by the reins, and he should not fall backwards or forwards when the horse changes gait. To obtain this independent seat takes a lot of practise, and a lot of riding. The most important thing in the beginning, however, is for the novice to get a feel for balance; this is not very different from finding your balance on the saddle of a bicycle or a motorbike.

The correct position. Insets show correct positioning of the foot.

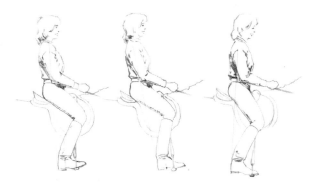

Correct seat   Chair seat   Fork seat

It should be mentioned that an independent seat can only be learned on a really well-schooled horse.

If you do not learn to sit correctly on the horse, you will never be able to ride well. Anyone who takes the trouble can learn to sit on a horse. It is *how* you learn to sit which matters. There are all sorts of faults you can develop, and bad habits you get into at the beginning will prove impossible to correct later. Hence, in riding, the correct seat is the basis for all that follows, just as the foundations are the basis for a house. If the foundations are not sound, it matters not how fine the bathroom is — the whole lot will eventually collapse.

21

The Seat in Walk, Trot and Canter

The Walk

It is understandable that a beginner does not want to spend time doing lots of exercises. He wants to get on, so that eventually he can go out on a hack with his horse, and enjoy riding through woods and fields. However, the gods have decreed that nothing shall be achieved without work – even in riding. It is impossible to spend too much time on those early exercises. You will be thankful later on, when, because your seat is good, you have no serious problems learning the aids. If your seat is faulty, you will have nothing but problems throughout the training which follows.

Nowadays, three different seats are recognised, each of which can be used in any of the three gaits. They are the dressage seat (where the rider remains seated in the saddle), the light seat (where the seat is just above the saddle with the upper body inclined forward) and the jumping, or forward, seat. The rider must master all three seats. However, it is much easier for a beginner to distinguish between the different seats if they are discussed in relation to each individual gait, even if this involves some repetition.

In walk – at least when doing flat work (dressage riding) in the school – the dressage seat is nearly always used. Only when riding out can the light seat occasionally be used.

When a horse comes into the school, he should, first, be ridden round the school a few times with loose side reins (which the horse should wear for the beginner's first few lessons), and 'on a long rein'. This entails holding the reins at a length which will allow the horse to carry his head and neck where he will. These circuits of the school at the beginning serve to de-contract the horse, to loosen him up after many hours spent in the stable. They are like the loosening-up exercises performed by an athlete prior to a training session, when he skips around and shakes his arms about. A beginner's horse will usually have been ridden and loosened up by another rider already, but, if the horse has just come out of the stable, after a few circuits of the school the girth will have to be checked.

In walk, if you really concentrate, you will feel every movement of each individual leg. A good rider can feel from the saddle the sequence of leg movements, though, naturally, a novice will be unable to do so at first. However, start by watching the horse's shoulders: when the right shoulder moves forward, the horse is bringing his right leg forward, etc.

It is in the walk that you first start to develop a feeling for balance in the saddle. The walk is the best gait for learning this because there is no risk of falling off, and any faults which

[91]

have crept in will not necessarily have dire consequences.

If possible, a novice rider should do a lot of work in walk. At many riding schools, unfortunately, they go too quickly into trot: the rider goes round a few times in walk, then trots, and then walks again. This is correct training, because you only really learn to ride by doing transitions from one gait to another in a progressive sequence, but there are many riders who have never progressed beyond the novice stage, and have given up riding altogether, because, at the beginning, they were not allowed the necessary time to acquire a feel for the balance. It is not a point which is in

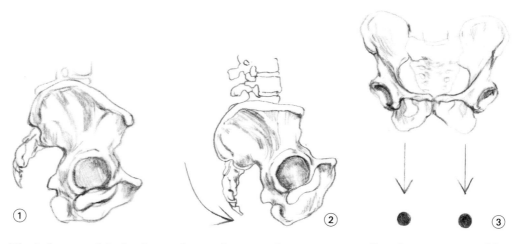

The influence of the back muscles on the seat: when you are standing the coccyx is in this position (1); when the back muscles are braced, the coccyx is pulled underneath (2); the same thing seen from in front (3).

Left: the rider's back muscles are braced. The weight and the coccyx act in a forwards/downwards direction.

Right: a hollow back has the opposite effect, the seat bones (and coccyx) are no longer in a position to act.

[92]

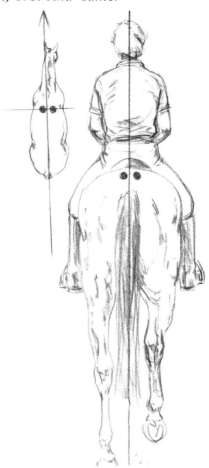

Sitting 'on one side': the horse is flexed to the right, with the rider sitting on the inside seat bone.

Sitting straight, with the horse straight. The weight is on both seat bones.

the rules, but every beginner should stay in walk until he has acquired a relatively secure feeling in the saddle.

In walk the aim is to sit on both seat bones, and to sit independently, that is, no 'gripping up' with the legs, no hanging on, and with the body free from tension and stiffness. The whole width of the seat should be in contact with the saddle, and the muscles should be free from contraction. As a beginner, you will, again and again, make the mistake of leaning too far forward because you are inexperienced and afraid

of falling off. After a few lessons, however, you will have gained your confidence, you will be fairly sure that the horse is not going to buck because he has not done so so far, and you will relax and stop leaning forward.

As your leg muscles stretch and become less tense, you will have the feeling that your legs are getting longer and longer. When you reach this stage, you realise that, at the beginning, the stirrups were actually too short. Unfortunately, however, the first time you experience this feeling is always in the

Beginners (and experienced riders too) learn
to sit correctly by riding without stirrups.

middle or at the end of the lesson, and
the next time you ride, you will find,
at least to start with, that the muscles
have contracted and the stirrups feel
too long again.

In later lessons, when you no longer
have side reins you should not, as a
novice, be too concerned if, while performing figures in walk, the horse fails
to maintain the correct position. To
insist that he do so would be asking
too much of you at this stage.

The Rising Trot

As has already been mentioned, the rising trot is the most comfortable and the least tiring gait, although some horses are easy to ride in trot, while others are difficult. The trot is a two-time movement, and the rider has the feeling that the horse's back is going up and down in time with the two beats. We say that the horse pushes the rider out of the saddle, and some horses do so more powerfully than others.

The novice will ride only in working trot initially. Working trot is similar to the collected trot, except that it lacks the engagement and collection,

and is therefore a little faster than the collected trot.

The rhythm of the trot can only be mastered on the lunge bacause the beginner is so busy adapting to the rhythm that he cannot manage to keep the horse going as well. Every beginner should have a few lunge lessons, with plenty of rising trot, before he tries to perform this exercise off the lunge.

Rising trot is actually quite simple. The rider sits in the saddle for one of the two trot beats, raises himself slightly out of the saddle for the second, and then sits down again — and so on. With experience the rider will

Changing the diagonal while changing the rein in rising trot. The rider remains seated for an extra step.

[96]

rise from the knee, which should be 'closed' against the saddle but not gripping it. To start with, however, the rider will rise from the stirrup, because in the beginning, he will be unable to keep his lower leg (i.e. from the knee down) still, and his hands will make exaggerated up and down movements in time with his body movements. The rising will also be exaggerated and uneven. All these are minor faults that will be corrected in time when the rider establishes a good rhythm. The important thing is to find this rhythm. The instructor with help by counting out loud 'one, two, one, two' ... On 'one' you rise, and on 'two' you sit down again.

When working in the school (out hacking it is not so important) you rise in time with the horse's inside hind leg. When the inside hind foot is put down, so is the outside foreleg (the horse's outside shoulder comes back), and the rider sits down. The outside foreleg and inside hind leg together are known as the 'outside diagonal'. Put another way, when the outside foreleg (or the shoulder) swings forward, the inside hind leg does so simultaneously, and the rider rises out of the saddle. ('Outside' means the side of the horse which is closest to the wall; 'inside' means the side which faces the middle of the school.)

The term 'wrong diagonal' means that the rider is sitting down in time with the horse's outside hind leg, i.e. with the wrong hind leg. This fault can be corrected simply by sitting for one more beat, and then rising.

[97]

The Sitting Trot

It is when the novice sits to the trot for the first time that he realises nothing is more difficult to sit than the sitting trot.

It is very easy to describe: the horse trots, and the rider remains seated in the saddle, but it is more easily said than done. When speaking of rising trot, we mentioned that the trot is a two-time gait, and that the horse's back goes up and down. In rising trot, the rider avoids the effects of the upward pushing movement by rising with each stride (every two beats). In sitting trot you can no longer avoid the upward movement.

The horse's back is the link between forehand and hindquarters — a bridge, as it were. Through gymnastic training of the horse, this bridge is made to 'swing'. However, it does not do so until the horse has been loosened up, and is free from tension, i.e. when the horse is in 'natural self-carriage'.

A 'soft' trot also depends on certain other things, the main one of which is the horse's conformation (construction). Horses which have elastic gaits have a naturally soft trot. Horses which are built 'uphill' are easier to sit than horses which are built 'downhill'. By 'uphill', we mean that the horse has his hindquarters well underneath his body (towards his centre of gravity), and so carries himself a bit higher in front. This enables the rider to sit 'uphill' and to have 'a lot more horse in front of him'. Horses have, by nature, more or less ability to engage their hind legs under their body, but good training can bring about considerable improvement in this respect. A well-trained horse should be thoroughly loosened up in walk, rising trot and canter before the rider begins sitting trot.

The horses usually used for teaching people to ride are, on the whole, not all that they should be. This cannot be helped, because, every day, they have several beginners banging around on their backs, hanging onto the reins, and giving the wrong aids. They are usually no longer as loose and supple as a good horse should be, nor do they really swing in their backs. Nevertheless, school horses should be as comfortable and as easy to sit as possible.

When you first sit to the trot you should simply try to accompany the horse's movements softly with the back and pelvis, and to sit deep into the saddle. You should sit upright, although, to start with, there is no harm in leaning back a little with the upper body slightly behind the vertical. This is not, strictly, correct, but it makes it easier to stay in the saddle and to sit into the trot movements. Try to be as supple and as free of tension as possible, not gripping up

with the knees or lower legs, and on no account seeking support from the reins. All this will certainly not be easy at first, you will keep falling into a crooked position, the horse will tend to throw you out of the saddle every second stride, and the whole thing will look more like an ungainly dance than a sitting trot. This is not important, and you should not allow yourself to be discouraged by it. Practice makes perfect.

If he has not already done so, the rider will realise during the first lessons of sitting trot that riding also involves fitness — not only that of the horse, but his own too. Twice around the school in sitting trot is enough to bring thick beads of sweat to the brow, and to make the hair under his riding hat damp. Then it is not long before the cry of 'Enough!' brings proceedings to a close.

Sportsmen and people who do proper fitness training have no problems, but most novice riders do not fall into these categories, so get into training yourself. Just a jog through the woods or the park two or three times a week plus a few exercises in the morning will be a great help. When you get back into the saddle in better shape, the world will seem a different place.

To sit to the trot, sit deep into the saddle with the lower legs lying close to the horse's sides, but not gripping up.

The Canter

Sitting securely in canter is not particularly difficult, but canter should not be commenced until the rider has achieved some degree of steadiness in the saddle. There is a simple reason for this: without it, the rider will fall off!

Before beginning canter, a psychological barrier has to be broken down: the canter and gallop are traditionally associated with whirlwinds, storms and wild flight. This gives the impression that the canter must be dreadfully difficult to learn, or downright dangerous. Of course, this is not the case; the canter is simply one of the horse's gaits, nothing more than this, and it is much easier to sit than the trot. All you need is a little practise, and to get used to the feel of the faster movement.

Two kinds of seat in canter are recognised: the dressage seat, and the light seat. The dressage seat is used for dressage-type training and riding, i.e. usually in the school. The light seat is used for riding outside, for jumping, for loosening up, and when riding young horses, because it places less weight on the horse's back. However, before learning the light seat, the dressage seat should be used, in order to give the rider some feel for this new gait.

Some practise in canter on the lunge is almost essential, because a beginner is not usually in a position to put the horse into canter, keep him there, and at the same time concentrate on his position. The riding instructor will choose a particularly quiet horse for this work on the lunge, and will fit him with side reins. This is the best way to give the student – first without reins – the chance to get the feel of the canter.

The canter gives the feeling of a round, forward, pushing movement. The rider has the impression that the horse's back moves downwards, and then swings forward and upward in

The light seat in canter (weight off the horse's back).

Canter using the dressage seat (sitting canter).

a long, semicircular movement. The rider must try to follow this movement in a way that is best described as wiping the saddle from back to front with the seat.

It is important in canter to have the knees right against the saddle. This should also be the case in walk and trot, but, to start with, they tend to keep coming away and losing contact with the saddle. The novice will not stay in the saddle for long if his knees are 'open', so, knees on!

In the light seat, which is only attempted after gaining some measure of proficiency in the dressage seat, the rider sits 'above' the saddle, so it is even more important to have the knees against the saddle. The legs are against the horse, the knees are closed, and the seat is raised just above the saddle, with the upper body inclined slightly forward. The horse is cantering along underneath you — or, at least, this is what it feels like.

Knees against the horse (closed), seat just above the saddle (light seat).

22

The Leg Position

Having explained the seat, we shall now go on to explain the legs – or rather, the position of the legs.

The instructor will keep on saying that the rider's stirrups are too short, and the rider will keep protesting inwardly (or even out loud) that the stirrups are much too long, his legs keep flapping about all over the place and he cannot keep them still. In fact, the stirrups usually *are* too short, but it takes time for the rider to realise it.

The rider's legs must hang long against the horse's sides – as long as possible. To start with, the beginner sits on top of the saddle, that is, he stiffens slightly because he is afraid and feels insecure, and does not sit with his seat supple and covering the whole surface of the saddle. Not until he relaxes, and brings his pelvis down

into the saddle (in riding language: 'sits deep into the horse'), will he notice that his stirrups are actually too short. As time goes on, and he develops a deeper, more relaxed seat, and his muscles become less tense, his legs will become 'longer and longer'.

The best way to achieve this length of leg is to do some work without stirrups. The stirrups are crossed in front of the saddle on the horse's shoulders – here they will not get in the way of horse or rider. With the legs hanging down unsupported against the horse's body, it is no longer possible to push yourself out of the saddle. Even a beginner then notices how long his legs are. After riding round the school a few times without stirrups, every student will find that he can lengthen his stirrups by a hole or two.

It is the inside of the thighs, knees, calves and ankles that lie against the horse's sides, not the back of the legs. The feet lie parallel with the horse's sides, and the balls of the feet rest on the stirrup iron. The heels should be a little lower than the toes, but this should be because of natural flexion in the ankle joints. If the heels are forced down the resultant leg position will be stiff, and the lower leg may be pushed forward. If the legs are in the correct position at halt, an imaginary vertical line can be drawn from shoulder to hip to heel. The lower leg position alters slightly when aids are applied.

Fundamentally, there are two places
where leg aids are applied: on the
girth and behind the girth (dotted line).

[103]

23

The Connection with the Horse's Mouth: The Reins

Fingers closed: the reins cannot slip through, and so cannot yield.

Fingers open: the reins can slip easily through the fingers (allowing the horse to take the rein downward: a long rein).

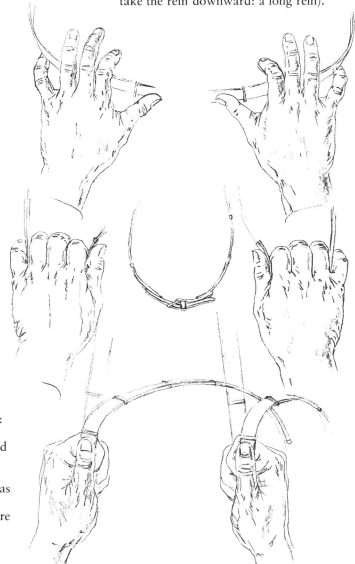

How to pick up the reins: the reins lie between the third and little fingers, and the excess rein comes out over the forefingers, with the thumbs on top acting as 'brakes' to stop the reins from slipping when they are not required to do so.

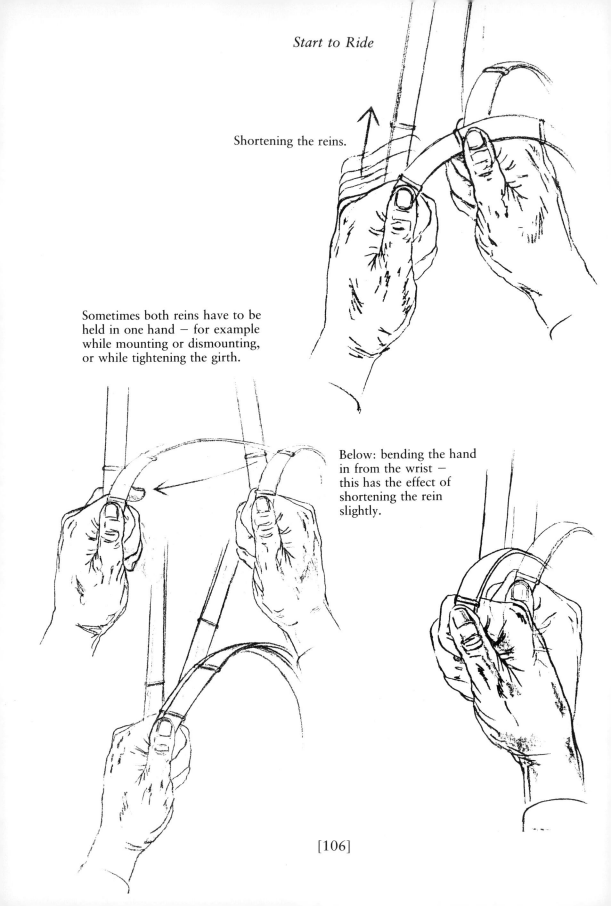

Shortening the reins.

Sometimes both reins have to be held in one hand – for example while mounting or dismounting, or while tightening the girth.

Below: bending the hand in from the wrist – this has the effect of shortening the rein slightly.

The outside rein is used to bring the horse into position. The inside rein is, as it were, the pivot, or fixed point, around which the outside rein moves. Unfortunately, the outside rein is sadly neglected – and not only by novices. When the pivot is not fixed, the outside rein has no anchor point around which to move.

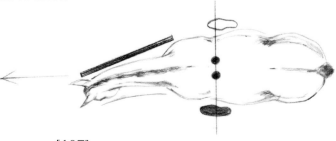

24

Every Rider is Also a Trainer

It takes a long time to train a tennis player. He may become a champion one day, but very few champions actually go on to train new tennis players. It is the same with footballers. A rider, on the other hand, becomes a horse trainer from the moment he finds himself sitting alone on the horse without side-reins or other auxiliary reins.

A horse used for teaching beginners ought to know considerably more than his rider, and yet even this horse is being trained by his rider because every time a horse is being ridden he is being trained. Of course, this training is not necessarily constructive; it can just as easily be negative.

They say that once you have learned to ride a bicycle, you never forget it, but if you get back on a bicycle for the first time for twenty years, you will certainly have some teething troubles, and will have to re-establish your balance and cycling ability. It is the same with a horse. If he has been well trained, but not ridden for some time, he will not have forgotten most of the exercises, but he must be reintroduced to the work by use of the appropriate aids to remind him of his early lessons.

The horse must also be brought to a level of fitness which will enable him to cope with the work because, just like people who have given up a certain sport, horses lose muscle, grow stiff, and become unfit.

Horses on which novices are taught are singled out by two things: firstly, they have to have calm, even temperaments; secondly, it is always very difficult to train them to a high level, because, whatever a good trainer does to improve the horse, will be undone as soon as a few beginners have ridden him. The result of this vicious circle is that the horse rarely, if ever, makes any progress in his training. This is also the unfortunate reason why it is the not very talented horses who are turned into school horses, despite the fact that, in the interests of the novice rider, school horses should be easy to ride and particularly well trained. Apart from the few exceptions to this rule, it has to be said that this is not the case.

After being ridden for a few days by beginners, a school horse should be 'tuned up' by an experienced rider using the correct aids because those given by beginners are not accurate. This should be standard practice but, again, it is the exception. In many riding schools, the school horses are rarely ridden by experienced riders. They are continually ridden, for better or for worse, by beginners which tends to have a deadening effect on them; they hardly recognise the correct aids any longer, and rely on the instructor's voice to guide them. When they hear the long drawn out 'Terr-ot', they start trotting, without waiting for the riders to work out what aids are required to make the horse trot on. This situation does, perhaps, help a novice rider to get the feel for the trot, and to practise going into trot, while concentrating more on himself than on the horse, but, in the long run, you cannot learn to ride in this way.

Every aid a beginner gives a horse is, therefore, a small piece of training, and is stored in the horse's memory, even if, as mentioned before, the training is negative. For example, if a horse is continually given inaccurate aids supported perhaps by the instructor's voice and, maybe, a whip, he will become programmed to respond only to these things. Should he be ridden at some stage by an experienced rider he will be confused by the aids this rider gives even though they are correct. How is the horse to know the previous aids were wrong?

It must be remembered, however, that although I state that every rider is a trainer, only an experienced rider should train a young inexperienced horse.

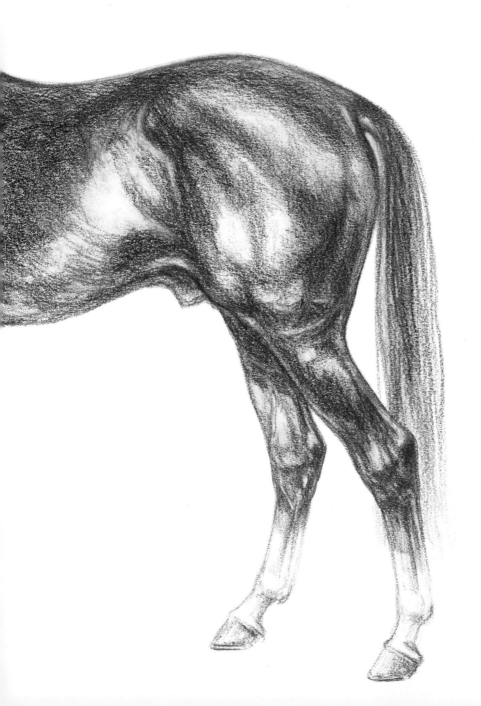

25

Gymnastic Training

Almost every student at the beginning of his riding career stands at the fence of the dressage arena and watches, shaking his head slightly, as the riders put their horses through the exercises. 'I wouldn't want to ride in such an unnatural way' they say, 'I shall steer clear of all this artificial flexion. I want the horse to go under saddle as it does in the wild.'

The rider who says this is wrong. He is also wrong when he says that dressage forces the horse into unnatural contortions, but that jumping fences in the woods and fields is in keeping with his nature, because, in fact, the opposite is true. All the movements performed in classical dressage form part of the behaviour of every horse, even in the wild. For instance, when a stallion is courting a mare, he performs piaffe and passage, and may show a levade, which we only know from high school work. Jumping, however, is only performed by horses in the wild if there is no alternative.

We must remember that horses were not designed by nature to carry people on their backs. From many centuries of riding history we know that they are, however, very well suited to the task — but only after appropriate training, and they must be trained in such a way that they can carry a rider without sustaining injury.

A young horse must first learn to regain his balance when carrying the additional weight of a rider. To begin with, the horse will position his hind legs slightly further apart, because this enables him to counterbalance the rider's weight more easily. As training progresses, however, the horse copes better with this weight.

If a horse has not been ridden for a long time he must relearn how to do this with the help of the necessary gymnastic exercises, just like a person who wants to do a handstand again after a twenty year break.

Hence the many exercises we perform with horses in the dressage arena are not an end in themselves. They are necessary for safe riding both in and out of the school. The basis of all forms of equitation is gymnastic training, or dressage, as it can also be called.

The horse's different muscles and groups of muscles are developed according to use. For example, the hindquarter muscles of a broodmare, who takes only a little gentle exercise in the field, are much less developed than the same muscles in a competition horse. Even someone who knows nothing about horses can appreciate the difference immediately. For the broodmare, the development of the hindquarter muscles is quite adequate, but it would take several months training, during which these muscles would be prepared for the increased demands, before this same mare could be entered in a competition. If entered before the muscles are built up, she would not put up a very good show. One of the main reasons for the unedifying spectacles seen at some shows (apart from the rider's lack of sound training), is that horses are entered when they are not ready, and asked to do things which, through lack of preparation, they are unable to do. This is like a Sunday afternoon sportsman taking part in the Olympics.

The suburban gymnast, who works out once a week to keep fit, knows that it is out of the question for him to take part in the Olympics. The horse, however, cannot make this decision. The gymnast will stop immediately he realises that his preparation and training are not sufficient for a set exercise, but horses are ridden hard across difficult country, sometimes when completely unfit, and it takes a knowl-

edgeable horsemen to realise they have been pushed far beyond their limits. It is nothing short of cruelty to push a horse to do an exercise for which he is not prepared — and this includes a long ride across country. It may be argued that, in the wild, horses were constantly on the move, and even covered long distances in trot and canter. However, we have already explained that a horse with the weight of a rider on his back is being asked to perform in quite different circumstances. One further point: in the wild, horses are automatically in training from an early age. Even as foals they learn to cover long distances, and so develop fitness and muscle. Yet how can a horse do this if he is standing in a stable for twenty-three hours of the day?

The gymnastic training of the horse is simply a substitute for what happens automatically in the wild. No human gymnast, even if trained to Olympic standard, would begin his workout with advanced exercises on the apparatus or on the floor. He would be afraid of straining tendons, ligaments or muscles. The same applies to horses — even top level competition horses. A human athlete will do some loosening exercises to start with, to stretch tendons and ligaments, and warm up the muscles through light work. Likewise, horses should first be given loosening exercises. Only after this loosening phase can the the horse be asked to perform the 'collected' exercises in which the muscles are taut.

Gymnastic exercises only look good when they are performed by well trained gymnasts — they look easy and almost effortless. Riding is only an enjoyable experience on a horse who has had proper gymnastic training and has been properly prepared for the exercises required of him.

26

Riding Circles

The circle is something the rider comes in contact with right at the beginning of his training, but he will probably not have given it a great deal of thought. As far as he was concerned, the horse he rode on the lunge when he was learning how to sit, was simply going round in circles. However, if he had paid more attention, he would have noticed that the side reins were adjusted in such a way that the horse's neck, head and even the body were bent slightly to the inside. After the lunge lessons, horse and rider worked mainly on the outside track, that is, around the edge of the arena.

The 20 m circle is the first school figure a young horse or a novice rider will learn when they come off the lunge. This circle runs around half (one end) of the arena. On the circle, the horse should be slightly bent along the whole of his longitudinal axis; it is not sufficient for head and neck alone to be bent inwards. This bending is one of the main elements of the horse's gymnastic training, and the circle provides an easy starting point for this work. It prepares the horse for the more pronounced bends which will be required of him later. With the bending, the rider begins to work, place demands on, and develop the horse's muscles.

When working on the circle the rider should adjust to this bend, he cannot sit symmetrically. The inside leg needs to be against the girth, and the outside leg about one hand's breadth behind it. There should be more weight on the inside seatbone than on the outside one. The outside hand yields more, and is therefore further forward, and the inside hand is very slightly further back.

Circles are ridden in all three gaits, though galloping is obviously not possible owing to the bend. Circles teach the horse to carry himself in canter, to engage his quarters more in this faster gait, and to move in a rounded outline. The rider must always ensure that it is a true circle, since there are only three reference points on the outside track to guide him – on the short side, and on each of the long sides. As the horse moves across the centre of the school there is no school wall or marker to help the rider with his accuracy. Beginners often ride around the outside track, and then, after a few strides along the long side, turn in towards the centre. A true bend throughout the length of the horse's body can only be ensured if the circle is ridden correctly.

Riding a correct circle.

27

The Lateral Movements

The lateral movements are the beginning of the real gymnastic training, and the novice rider will find it very difficult at first to make his horse step sideways.

Why do we perform lateral work? This perfectly reasonable question must be answered with another question: why does a human gymnast try to do the splits, or why does he perform a 'candle' or a handstand even though he intends to work on the rings or on the bars and not perform floor exercises? The reason, of course, is that he is using these preparatory exercises to train his muscles for the task ahead. With horses, the lateral movements are used for this same purpose of preparation.

Most horses have a slight natural bend, and do not, therefore, move quite straight. There are numerous theories as to why this should be so. The commonest and probably the most logical of these is that the foal lies in a bent position for about eleven months in his mother's womb, thus giving rise to the slight crookedness present in the young horse. Some horses — in fact, most of them — are bent slightly to the left, while others are bent to the right. The ratio of right to left bend is probably the same as in foals in the womb.

The rider must try to straighten the young horse's natural crookedness through training. Obviously, a horse who is slightly bent to the left finds it preferable and easier to go round on the left rein (to the left), so he should be ridden on the left rein initially. However, since the horse must be able to work equally well on either rein, not only must he be straightened by judicious exercise, but also a good right bend must be developed. With horses who are naturally bent to the right, the opposite applies.

Once the young horse has been made straight, the lateral work can begin. The idea is that horses who usually only go straight forward, learn through the lateral work to use and develop other muscles which can be utilised in situations other than just forward movement — for example, when negotiating a steep slope, or jumping a fence.

The leg-yield is usually the first of the lateral movements to be taught. The horse must literally yield to the leg, that is, he should move sideways away from the rider's leg in response to the pressure of the leg on his side. The rider sits upright and positions the horse so that his head is at a slight angle to the wall. This means that the horse is travelling on two tracks: his forelegs are on the normal track, while the hind legs are on another track.

The rider's weight is then transferred to the inside, the inside leg becomes active, and is brought back towards the hindquarters, while the outside leg is placed behind the girth

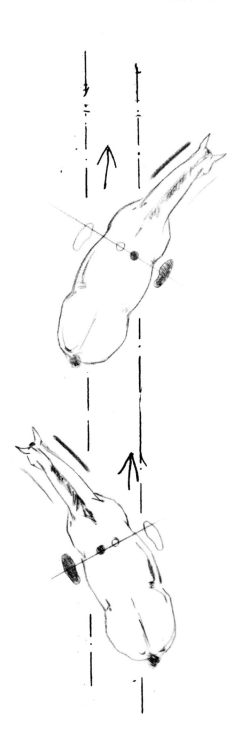

in a 'guarding' or 'supporting' role (with the heels remaining low). The horse's head and neck should be bent only very slightly to the inside. The inside rein has a 'guarding' or 'supporting' function, while the outside rein 'leads' the horse to the side.

After a while, the same exercise should be performed with the horse's head pointing to the centre of the school. Leg-yielding makes the horse supple, and teaches him to respond to the lateral aids (aids acting on one side). Leg-yielding is particularly important and beneficial for the novice rider because it allows him to feel how the different aids interact to give one result.

After a few lessons of leg-yielding along the wall, the rider will be asked to leg-yield inwards from the wall. In Germany this exercise is called 'making the school smaller' which is a good way of explaining what happens. The school is a large rectangle. Going along on the outside track entails riding a large rectangular shape. However, you can also ride a smaller rectangular shape by riding further away from the walls. One way of doing this is to ride on the inside track.

Hence if you are riding on the outside track, and you then use the leg-yield exercise to make the horse step sideways and inwards, you are decreasing the size of the rectangle you are riding around. When you leg-yield outwards, or 'make the school larger', you are making the rectangle bigger by moving outwards.

The novice rider should learn leg-yielding first because, of all the lateral movements, it has the easiest aids, plus it gives the rider the feel of the horse moving away from the leg. In time leg-yielding can be followed by the more advanced lateral movements including shoulder-in, renvers (quarters-out)

Leg-yielding to the inside (top) and to the outside (below).

Leg-yielding

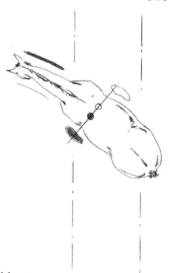

and travers (quarters-in).

All these lateral movements are ridden in walk at first. Not until later are they ridden in trot — and then for only short periods, since they place a lot of strain on the horse.

Shoulder-in

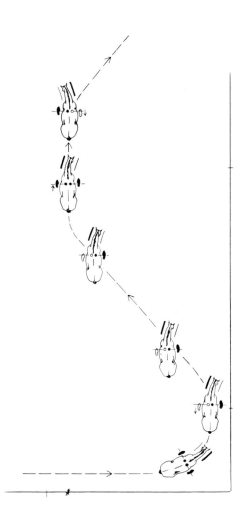

Travers, or quarters-in (top) and renvers, or quarters-out (below)

28

What is a Halt?

Starting and stopping a car is easy; when you put your foot on the accelerator it goes forward, and when you put your foot on the brakes it slows down or stops. No car driver would dream of using the accelerator and the brakes at the same time, but that is in effect how you slow down or stop a horse, but more about this later.

These are two types of halt, the half halt and the (full) halt. Let us, first, clarify what the different expressions mean. The half halt is a transitionary or regulatory exercise, and the halt is when the horse comes to a stop. The half halt is used to make a horse who is rushing go more slowly, to bring a horse from trot to walk, to improve the carriage in a given gait, to alert the horse to the next exercise, and to shorten the trot or walk. The halt, as all ready stated, actually beings the horse to a standstill.

To begin with, every novice rider

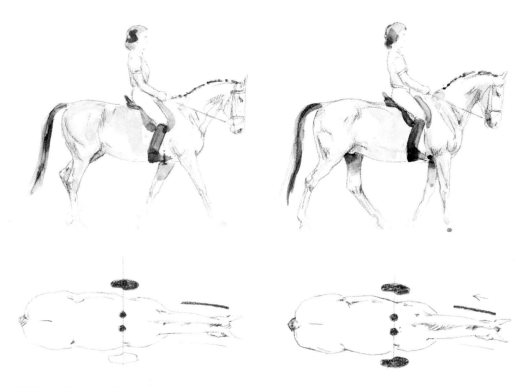

Full halt from walk

finds it completely incomprehensible that he should have to apply the brake and the accelerator simultaneously. If it is any consolation, many advanced riders are also unclear on the theory, although they have learnt the exercise correctly, and also perform it correctly.

It is worth trying to explain this theory with an example. Think of the parachute-drag braking system used on a jet fighter plane. The parachute is attached to the back of a fast aeroplane, and brought into action the moment the plane touches down. The air rushes into the parachute and inflates it, bringing about a considerable increase in braking power. However, if the parachute were not attached to the back of the plane, it would have no effect. Logically, it must be secured in order to inflate, and so effect a braking action.

Halts, and half halts, work on a similar theory; you need the forward impulsion to be able to brake. Let us take, for example, a horse performing working trot. The rider wishes to change down a gear to walk. It is true that many school horses can be slowed down just by pulling on the reins, perhaps with a little help from the voice, but this has little to do with equitation. The horse should not alter his carriage, and should perform the transition fluently and without resistance, and without the rider pulling on the reins.

In the half halt, the rider increases his leg pressure, braces his back muscles, and at the same time tightens the reins. He resists, so to speak, while at the same time he causes the hind legs to step more under the body, and in this way pushes the horse onto the bit. The horse feels the resistance of the bit in his mouth, the rider continues

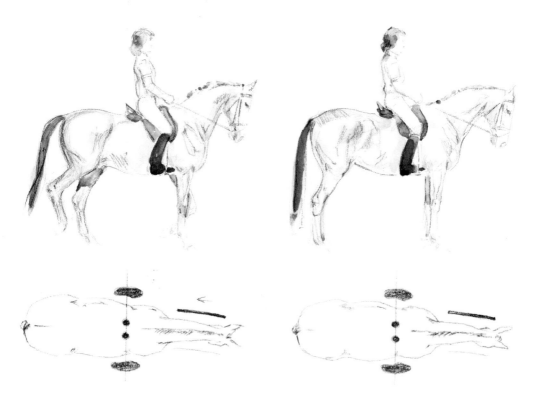

to resist with the reins for a short time, and then yields. At this point the horse goes into walk.

It looks easy enough on paper! Obviously, in reality it is not so simple. It is the halts and half halts which distinguish the rider who is a 'natural' from one who is not. For this exercise you need 'feel', and the ability to react differently from one situation to the next. You cannot learn halts and half halts with your head. All you can do is understand what you are doing every time you perform one. In every situation, and with each different horse, and especially with every single halt or half halt, the aids have to be adjusted.

No beginner will succeed straight away with his half halts, and you should not fool yourself into thinking that it will suffice to start with if you just resist with your hands (you will undoubtedly have to pull back slightly on the reins), however, as long as you do not make a habit of it, it can be forgiven in the early stages. Even good riders, in many situations, and especially on certain horses, need to perform repeated half halts to achieve their aim, or until the half halts 'come through' as we say. A very well-schooled horse will accept a half halt much more quickly than a less well-schooled one.

The full halt is performed in exactly the same way as the half halt. The

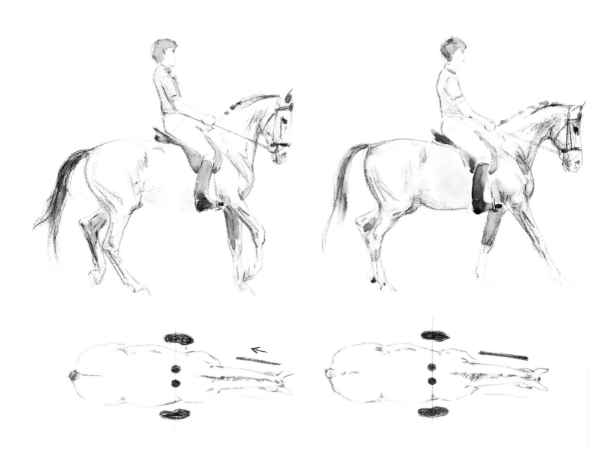

Half halt from trot to walk

only difference is that the aids are usually more intensive. The aim of a full halt is to come to a standstill from whatever gait you might be working in, and can be performed more easily on a straight line. They too may have to be repeated several times to achieve the desired result.

At the beginning of the lesson the horse is not yet loosened up, or is not completely worked in, and so the halts and half halts will not 'come through' as well as they would with a supple horse.

If the horse is working in trot, and needs to be brought back to a walk by use of a half halt – or several half halts – the rider braces his back muscles and increases his leg aids. The reins are tightened – drawn back – slightly, the horse 'comes up against the bit' and his forehand becomes a little higher. As soon as he decreases the tempo, that is, as soon as he accepts the half halt, the reins yield very slightly. The driving aids are maintained until the horse has made the transition into walk, and is striding forwards in a good position and good carriage.

When all that is needed is to bring the horse to attention in preparation for a different exercise, the half halt is performed a little less strongly. The driving aids are not so pronounced, and the reins resist only momentarily.

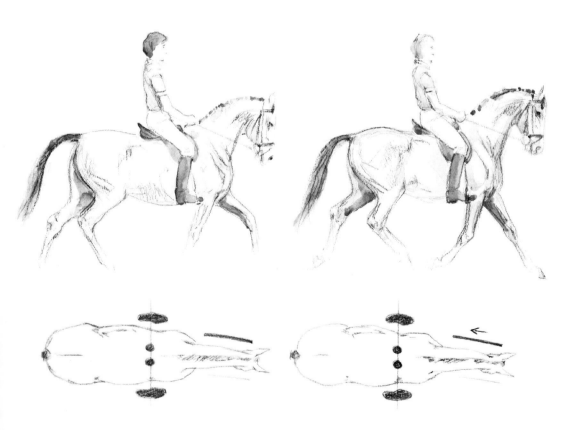

Half halt from canter to trot

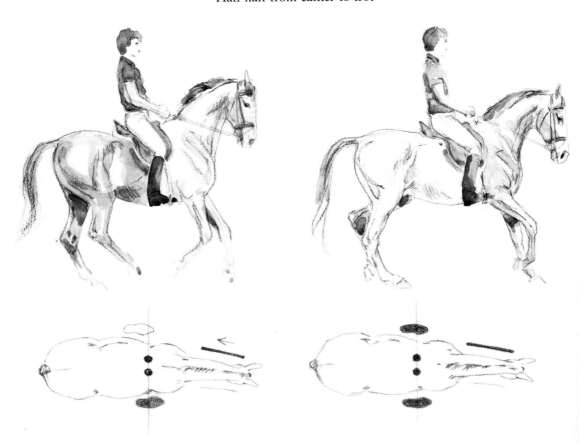

29

Freedom from Tension

How often we hear riding people use the words 'loose' and 'looseness', (loose in the sense of freedom from tension, supple but not slack) and yet how often their horses are tense and stiff. 'Letting yourself go' is a modern expression, but if applied to the horse, it could be said to express one of the important basic principles of classical equitation. German horsemen call this looseness *Losgelassenheit*. It is not confined to classical dressage: no form of riding anywhere in the world is possible without the looseness and freedom from tension of the horse — and of the rider.

We have already discussed the gymnastic training of the horse which serves to develop the muscles necessary for the horse to be able to perform the exercises.

No two horses are alike. Any beginner will have noticed this after just a few lessons. Some horses are soft to sit on, others are hard. This is to do with the horse's natural looseness, or lack of it. Their muscles are, by nature, differently developed, and they are built differently. One foal will already display great elasticity in his gaits at an early age, springing freely across the field, with a swinging back. Another will tighten his back and take tense strides. Looseness and freedom from tension will be much easier to achieve when it comes to training the first horse than in the case of the second one.

Yet no horse will be loose in the correct sense of the word just because he is naturally endowed with the necessary prerequisites. This is because, as we have already said, no horse was designed by nature to carry the weight of a rider. When a father lets his young son sit on his back, and walks around the living room carpet on all fours, he stiffens his back in order to carry the weight more easily. And if the child jumps up onto his back, his back muscles will still be tensed minutes afterwards as a result of the hard and unexpected landing of the weight on his back.

The same thing happens with horses. The rider's weight on his back causes the horse to tense his muscles in order to support this weight. Nervousness should also be considered. Every day we ask something new of our horse; he works in the school, in the outdoor dressage and jumping arenas, in the fields, and in many other places and situations which are new to him, causing him to tense up physically and mentally. Mental tension, in its turn, leads to more physical tension.

To be loose the horse must be completely free from contraction, with minimum tension throughout his body, and in his action. Schooling alone will not achieve this; the horse must overcome his early fears and develop confidence in his rider before the gymnastic training can begin.

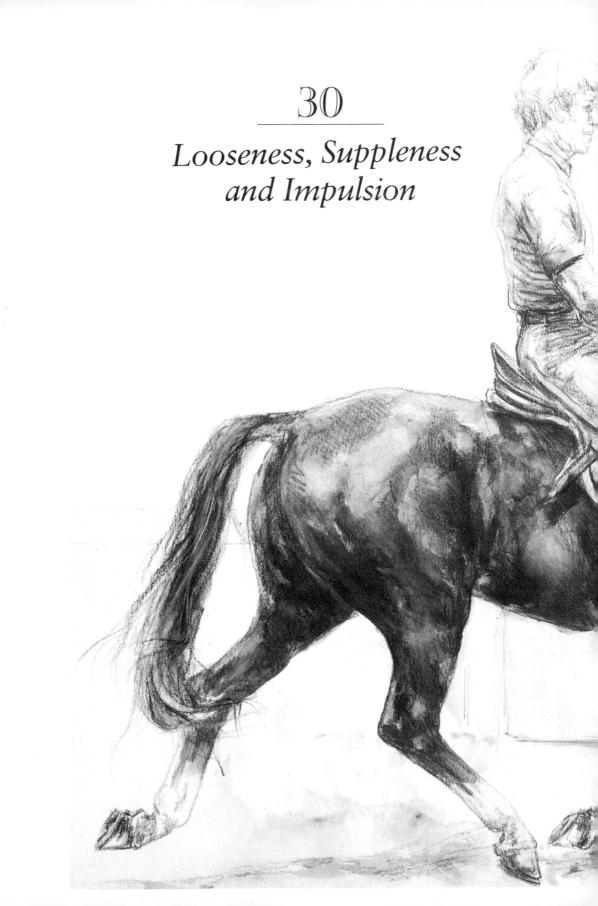

30

Looseness, Suppleness and Impulsion

31

Every Horse Has Rear-Wheel Drive

The horse's engine is at the rear, therefore, the power, which takes the form of pushing, comes from the rear. This is a basic principle which no rider should forget. In addition, the thrust which brings about movement comes from the hindquarters; it is developed in the hindquarters, and travels right through the horse's body to the forehand.

When an experienced horseman describes a horse as having his hind legs 'engaged', he means that the horse is in a position to develop a lot of forward thrust from the hindquarters. Horses which do not engage, or have not learned to engage, their hind legs can obviously not develop so much thrust. This sounds complicated, but it is actually quite simple.

To understand this exactly, you must go down on all fours. If you move your legs back slightly and then try to go forward, you will find that you cannot really get going, and even your hands can only make small 'strides'. However, if you bring your legs (the equivalent of the horse's hind legs) well under your body, you can develop much more power, and your hands too can go further. You will also notice that when you bring your legs underneath you your back slopes upwards towards the shoulders, 'uphill', as we call it. This is beneficial for the rider because it is much easier to sit on an 'uphill' horse than on a horse whose hind legs are trailing out behind.

We have already discovered that all horses are different. Some horses are built in such a way that their hind legs are naturally underneath them and, even as foals, these horses move with impulsion in an 'uphill' position. There are also horses who are physically incapable of adopting an 'uphill' position; a disadvantage because a horse who is naturally constructed 'uphill' will obviously be able to cope far better with the weight of a rider. Yet horses of varying levels of natural ability can be considerably improved in this respect by correct training. The aim of all schooling is to make the horse engage his hind legs more towards his centre of gravity, and so make it easier for him to carry the rider. The horse must first learn to flex his haunches — that is, his hindquarters. Again, this is something which can only be achieved through constant, correct training of the muscles in this region. Many of the dressage exercises which are learnt even during the rider's early lessons are aimed at this muscle training.

Every horse must retain his natural impulsion. What is more, this natural impulsion should be made even better through correct training. It is also possible, though, to destroy a horse's impulsion, to 'ride it out of him'. The gaits can be ruined through incorrect training. This happens when the horse is 'pulled together' and restricted, and not sufficiently 'loose'.

Many horses are 'on the forehand' when they are ridden. This is usually due to the rider's lack of skill, though sometimes simply to lack of knowledge. The first effect of this is that the rider cannot sit properly, the horse is in a 'downhill' position, the hindquarters develop hardly any thrust (because they cannot), and the forelegs perform a flat, usually shortened, trot. The second, but most important, effect is that excessive strain is placed on the forehand, and such horses are relatively prone to tendon and ligament trouble (if not worse). This way of going places a comparatively greater weight on the forehand — certainly more of the weight of the rider.

Many riders are against proper training, and simply swing themselves onto the horse's back in order to be carried around the countryside. This is a lovely idea, but these horses must obviously be on their forehand, because their backs have not been developed to carry the weight of a rider. It is quite simply impossible to place a weight of 50–80 kg. on a horse's back without preparing the horse beforehand. Unfortunately, most of these riders have no idea what 'on the forehand' means, and do not realise how much damage they are doing to their horses in this way.

It is nice, and desirable, that more and more people are enjoying horses without having competitive ambitions, but people must understand that they are not doing the horse a kindness by letting him go around untrained with the rider simply sitting on his back. Even a horse required purely for hacking out must receive training. It is like driving a car around with no oil in the engine — it soon breaks down. If people do not wish to bother about horsemanship or the few concepts outlined here, but simply want to have horses around them, they should not be riding.

32

The Horse 'On the Bit'

During the first riding lessons, the rider's attention is focused on keeping his balance and not falling off. Next he tries to come to grips with the leg and weight aids. Then he goes to great pains to try to use the right amount of each aid, and to coordinate the aids as far as possible.

Of course, the classical school of horsemanship demands correct co-ordination of all the aids, and this is what must be taught, because, in principle, it is obviously right. In practice, however, it is almost impossible.

Every riding student should strive from the outset to combine the use of the weight, leg and rein aids, though he will not succeed. Some people learn quickly how to use their weight in the saddle, while others find the leg aids very easy from the outset.

The wrong leg aids — and indeed the wrong weight aids — confuse the horse, but they do not hurt him. Incorrect use of the rein aids, however, does hurt the horse. For this reason, a novice rider must learn that rein aids should be given sympathetically and

Horse 'on the bit'

always in conjunction with the leg and weight aids. To do this efficiently the rider needs a well-balanced and independent seat.

Novice riders use the expression 'on the bit' as if it had some magic quality: 'My horse came on the bit today'. It is rather like a young footballer scoring his first goal. The novice will have seen many horses in the school, ridden by advanced riders, who are on the bit – or so he thinks. In fact many of these horses only look as if they are on the bit. A strong person can hold a horse so tightly with the reins that he has to bring his head down, and thus gives the impression he is on the bit. You also find horses which get behind the bit. These horses, whose heads are so close to their chests that they look like they are biting themselves, also give the impression to the novice that they are on the bit. In neither case has the aim been achieved.

First of all we must clarify what is actually meant by the term 'on the bit'. The bit lies in the horse's mouth. It lies on the bars, which are the part of the gum where there are no teeth. The rings on the bit connect it to the ends of the two reins. Let us now imagine a good rider on the horse. This rider will first ride the horse on a long rein. He will loosen him up, using mainly leg and weight aids. The horse goes with his neck stretched, and the reins keep a light contact with his mouth. Through the use of the driving aids (legs and weight), the horse is then brought more 'together', that is, he is made to engage his hind legs more. After this phase, the rider puts the horse on the bit by using more driving aids, and slowly riding the horse onto the bit. The reins are shortened, and the hands remain still and supporting. The driving aids are continued, the horse's neck becomes

Horse on a long rein

more upright, and flexes more at the poll (behind the ears). The horse is, by now, mouthing the bit contentedly: he respects the contact and control. No force is used, and the arms are not tensed. The horse's nose should be slightly in front of the vertical, that is, when you look at the horse from the side, the line from the ears, through the forehead, to the nose, should slope forwards slightly, and not be quite vertical.

When the horse meets these conditions, he is said to be accepting a contact with the bit. The horse keeps, with his mouth, a contact with the soft hand of the rider by means of the connection through the bit and reins. If this contact is obtained through force, the horse is not really on the bit at all. On the contrary, as soon as the rider relaxes his pull for a second to start a different exercise, the horse will escape from this forced position. Things are just as bad when the horse gets behind the bit or behind the contact. When looked at from the side, the horse's neck is curled under, and the nose slopes backwards (behind the vertical). In this case the rider has no influence on the horse with the reins, because by curling his neck the horse breaks the contact between the rider's hand and the bit.

Only with a secure contact is it possible for the rider to bring his aids to act on the horse at any moment.

What the horse looks like when he is on the bit differs according to his level of training. Young horses are ridden forwards and downwards. The muscles in the neck which serve to

Horse on a loose rein

Older horses are more or less erect — or high in front — depending on the degree of engagement of the hind legs.

Obviously, it is not the carriage of the head and neck which determines whether the horse is on the bit or not. The rider must feel a steady, soft contact between the horse's mouth and his hands. This is even possible when the horse has his neck stretched. There have been numerous very successful showjumpers (especially in the U.S.A.) who have worked all the time with their necks long and extended, that is, not flexed, and yet they have been on the bit throughout, even over difficult courses of jumps.

support it are as yet undeveloped, and the horse must first learn to come into a more erect position and bring his hind legs further and further underneath his body. Nevertheless, it is still possible for a young horse, with his neck long and low, to be on the bit.

33

What is a Deep Seat?

The seat is the be all and end all for every rider. Once some degree of independence in the seat has been achieved, all the aids become considerably simpler and easier. The seat is the basis for all riding.

How to sit well in the saddle is not something you learn in a few months, or often even in years. If you work at it surely and steadily, and ask an instructor or some other good rider to put you through exercises on the lunge, you will notice how your seat improves continuously. However, if you think you are above this sort of thing, or think that you have a good seat once you are no longer in constant danger of falling off, you will never have the good fortune to be a really good rider.

It should also be said that the great riders — even Olympic and world champions — constantly ride on the lunge. Any rider, however excellent, must always be checking and improving his seat. As a rule, it is not possible to do this alone. The best thing for the novice is to keep riding on the lunge, preferably on a horse wearing side reins, to improve his seat.

Once you have learnt how to sit, or found your seat, as it were, in rising trot and in the light seat, the main concern is to improve your dressage seat. Here it is important to 'sit into the horse' as deeply as possible. For this you need long stirrups, legs which hang long and do not cling to the horse (grip up), because if you clamp your knees or lower legs against the horse, you cannot sit deep into the saddle, and both seatbones must be in contact with the saddle. To make it easier to achieve this, you should ride as often as possible without stirrups at all gaits. You notice immediately how much longer your legs become when they are not restricted by the stirrups.

First of all you should go round the school a few times in walk, and ride some figures. Later, you should do more and more work in trot. Gradually, also, you will become fitter, and the trot phases can be extended considerably.

Working without stirrups helps to achieve
a deep seat.

[137]

34

What Can a Horse Do?

During his early lessons no rider gives much thought to what a horse can do. When compared to man the horse seems to have almost unlimited powers, but this is not the case. It is very easy to ask too much of a horse.

Essentially, horses are creatures of flight, as we have established, and this kind of animal can obviously cover many miles in a day. To do this, however, he needs to be living in the wild, and so to have been undergoing natural intensive fitness training from an early age; or he needs to have been trained by man. Nowadays we keep our horses differently, and we also train them differently to some extent, yet even the horses we have in our stables today, assuming they are sound, are capable of walking quietly for 12 to 15 hours a day without coming to any harm. If we watch horses who are turned out day and night in the field, we see that they spend up to 20 hours a day walking about from one tuft of grass to another.

Even in trot, provided he has had some measure of physical training, a horse can cover many miles in a day. In times past, army horses covered an average of 63 miles a day, and on certain days managed, still in trot, almost 125 miles.

These were obviously particularly tough, fit horses, but what kind of trot would be used to cover these distances? Many miles can be covered in a rising, working trot, but a horse can maintain a medium trot or an extended trot, in the correct position, for only a few hundred metres, because of the strain involved. These gaits are reserved in the wild for extreme situations (e.g. a stallion courting a mare), and for short periods. The same applies to the canter and gallop. In the wild or in the field, the horse gallops very infrequently. He gallops when he thinks he has to run away from danger, and when he is excited. Excitement is usually connected with danger, or imagined danger, though it may also be caused by, for example, another horse being introduced into the herd. This sets them all off, because they need to defend their positions in the herd hierarchy. Horses also gallop out of exuberance and the sheer joy of living. When they are let out in the morning after a long night in the stable, they gallop around the field, bucking, simply because they are glad to be free again.

To decide what the horse is capable of, and what his limits are, we must refer to his level of training, or more precisely, to his level of physical training. It must not be forgotten that there is a psychological, as well as a physical aspect to the horse's performance, and the two sides cannot be separated, they work together. In this connection we speak of nervousness, temperament, courage and boldness.

If a horse is pushed beyond his limits, he may sustain not only serious physical injury, but also psychological damage, and this is often far more difficult to put right than a damaged tendon or other physical injury.

As with a young person taking up a sport, the demands on a young horse should be increased gradually, and he should be worked only for short periods at a time. Only after two or three years of physical and mental preparation may he be worked for longer periods. A well-trained school horse, under the expert supervision of an instructor, can be ridden by beginners for three to four hours a day.

Provided the horse is given the necessary breaks in walk and halt while the other riders are having their turn at the exercise, he will not come to any harm from being worked for this length of time. Unfortunately there are some riding schools where horses are worked for six or more hours per day. This is often the case with stables that offer 'horses for hire'.

Fitness must not only be built up, it must be constantly maintained. Horses are the same as people in this respect. If you leave the horse all week in the stable, or exercise him for only a short period each day, when it comes to the weekend, you cannot ride off, at a fast pace, for miles on end. It is no good making the excuse that the horse was out in the field all week. Only rarely does a horse keep himself fit in the field, for example, young stallions play high-spirited games and chase each other round the field. Adult horses, when turned out, do not move about much more than is necessary for grazing. Proper physical training, and the building up of fitness, can only be accomplished through the rider.

There are some external signs which can give some indication that the horse is under strain which the novice may find difficult to recognise at first.

You should not be misled by sweat; horses sweat quickly and profusely, particularly in summer. Almost no other animal sweats as much as a horse. A novice rider may also think that a horse is distressed when his nostrils are flared to take in as much air as possible, and his flanks are heaving and pumping at every breath. Usually, the horse soon recovers; the breathing should have returned to normal within a few minutes. However, if the horse is still like this after a quarter of an hour, it can be assumed that he is ill or has been pushed beyond his limits.

It should not be necessary to say this among true horsemen, but experience has shown that often it *is* necessary: no rider should get on a horse who he knows to be sick, exhausted or lame. If, whilst he is on the horse, he realises that this is the case, he should dismount immediately and lead the horse back to the stable — however far away this may be.

And the Fitness of the Rider?

'Riding is a leisurely sport: you sit yourself down in the saddle and let the horse carry you about!' This is often said by people who have never sat in a saddle. Once you have had a few lessons, you realise that riding is very demanding, as well as being associated, to start with, with aching muscles. The muscle pains pass after a few lessons, and do not recur provided you ride regularly (a break of approximately three weeks is about the limit). However, a rider always needs to be fit. Even before your first lesson, check your fitness. For the early lessons you do not need to have enough 'puff' to do a 5,000 m run, but neither should you be sweating and blowing at the third flight of stairs you have to go up.

If you are unfit, getting on a horse and trying to learn to ride is not much fun. Fitness can easily be tested, with a skipping rope for example. If you can manage ten to twenty jumps without stopping, and without finishing completely out of breath, you will be alright in the saddle. During the course of a lesson, if you are unfit, your concentration suffers after a while – and then everything goes. Anyone who really wants to learn to ride, and has not been particularly active in sport beforehand, should begin to improve his fitness during the same period that he starts his riding lessons. He will progress much faster with his riding, and will be doing himself a good turn in other ways too.

Running and swimming are good for building stamina and endurance. If you are unable to do either of these, at least do some work in the gym to get yourself fit for riding, but be sure not to overdo it! You can be excused an eight mile run through the woods just before your riding lesson, and swim-

[140]

ming just before riding is physically too demanding. There should be a break of at least a few hours between your fitness training and your ride.

Fitness builds up gradually, but even after a week you will notice the difference, and, when in the saddle, it will make all the difference in the world. However, once you are fitter, and, as a result, your body control is a little better, this does not mean that you are excused any further exercises in the saddle.

The first step, as with many things, is the hardest, and I speak from experience, so get started, give yourself a push. You will get a lot more fun out of riding if you are fit, and, especially at the beginning, you will not be forever despairing at your own clumsiness.

This advice is intended primarily for adult riders. Children and young riders are usually sufficiently fit and, above all, naturally supple. For them, fitness training usually assumes significance − and possibly becomes a necessity − only when they begin to ride competitively. However, some special riding exercises are recommended for both groups; they are designed to work on the parts of the body required for riding. Throughout these exercises, the seat should remain still in the saddle. There is a range of exercises aimed at making the hips as free and supple as possible. The simplest of these is rolling the hips, which should be practised a few times each day.

All exercises which train the leg muscles are useful. However, there is one in particular which uses those muscles which cause all the aches and pains during the early lessons. Place the legs slightly apart, with the feet parallel, now bend your knees so that you are in the riding position. Then, keeping the upper body upright, crouch down as low as you can, and then straighten up again, and so on. This exercise should be repeated as often as possible, and for as long as possible.

35

A Horse is Not a Football!

In a game of football, 22 players concentrate all their energies on playing for ninety minutes with a round, leather ball. The ball is the focal point of the whole game. Yet after the final whistle, no one bothers with the ball any longer. It is thrown carelessly into a corner. At best, someone takes pity on it before the next game, and rubs some leather dressing into it. If it is going down, it will be reinflated with a pump. A horse, however, is not a football.

The end of the lesson is far from being the end of the contact with the horse. Unfortunately, it has to be said that in many riding schools you find riders who leave the horse, still with his tack on, in the school, in the hands of a groom, so that they can go off and do other things. Among them are riders who have an excellent seats, and who perhaps have the shelves of their houses lined with glittering trophies which they show off proudly to visitors. However, these people are not good horsemen.

Anyone who is serious about horses (and this should mean all riders), should also be serious about 'horsemanship' in the broad sense of the word. This is a very English concept, as is 'fairness' − neither can be translated with complete accuracy into other languages. These two concepts have a lot in common. 'Horsemanship' could perhaps be defined as care of, and fairness towards, your partner the horse, and be developed into a creed and an unquestionable rule. A true horseman takes trouble over his riding, and then, afterwards, takes trouble over his horse. The horse comes first. The drink and the gossip must wait until the horse has been seen to.

No horse should be returned to his stable while he is still hot, or wet with sweat; he must always be walked until he is dry. Even if he has not actually been sweating, he still needs some time to wind down. He must be allowed to stretch after his exertions, and should at least be ridden around the school a few times in walk on a long rein. A particularly caring rider will walk his horse out of the school on a long rein and ride around quietly outside for a while. Care should be taken, however, because sweating horses can easily get cold in the wind. If there is a big difference between the inside and the outside temperature, the horse should not be taken out of the school straight away.

36

Back to the Stable

At the end of a lesson, and once the horse has cooled off, there are still a lot of jobs to be done before the rider can relax.

At the end of a lesson, and once the horse has cooled off, there are still a lot of jobs to be done before the rider can relax.

People who learn to ride on school horses who have to work for several hours each day, sometimes have little opportunity to take care of 'their' horse after they have ridden him, but every rider should learn as quickly as possible how to do this.

Before leaving the school, the girth is loosened; this in itself affords the horse some relief, but above all it tells him that the work is finished, and that he is about to go back to his stable.

First the horse must be unsaddled and this is done either in the stable or in an area designated for this purpose. The horse should either have his bridle removed and be tied up by the head-collar, or, if help is available, he can be held by the reins. The horse must never be tied up by the bridle. If he were to take fright and pull back, not only would he damage his mouth, but he could also damage or break the bridle, and bridles are not cheap.

Before removing the saddle, the stirrup irons should be run up the stirrup leathers to keep them out of the way, and the girth is undone on the left side and laid across the seat to prevent it being trodden on while the saddle is being carried. The saddle is then lifted off the horse's back carefully. A saddle is always handled with respect not only, again, because it is an expensive item, but also because the safety of horse and rider can sometimes depend on the saddle being in good condition. Once the saddle has been removed it should be taken straight to its saddle stand and not placed on the ground or dumped in the corner.

You should then look the horse over to see if there are any minor wounds, which need to be treated straight away. A common site for injuries is the coronet, which is the place where the foot joins the leg. Usually, these are just grazes which need to be disinfected. If you find a wound of this type, inform the instructor or the owner of the stables.

The feet are then picked out with the hoof pick, especially if you have been out hacking, because stones or other foreign bodies can become stuck or wedged in the foot and can lead to painful bruises. Horses' feet should be oiled or greased to keep them supple and promote the circulation. This is necessary nowadays because the feet of stable-kept horses do not retain sufficient moisture by natural means. In some stables the feet are oiled before riding, in others afterwards. Opinions differ as to how often the feet should be treated (daily is probably a bit too often), so find out how things are done at your stables, and follow their routine.

If the weather is suitable, and the horse is very sweaty, it is advisable to wash down the saddle area. On a very warm day, this can be done with a hosepipe, otherwise a sponge is used. Dried sweat can lead to saddle sores the next time the horse is ridden, and these can lay the horse off work for a long time.

The nostrils and dock (the area just under the base of the tail) should be wiped down, with two separate sponges, after the horse has been worked. If you are new to the stables, ask which sponges are used for these jobs.

In many stables (except in the heart of winter) the horses' legs are hosed down. This is done for two reasons. Firstly, this serves to remove any dirt and mud after the horse has been ridden, especially across country. Secondly, the cold water cools the tendons after work, and also has a massaging effect.

When the back has been washed down, excess water is removed with a sweat scraper, and, after hosing, the legs are wiped down with the hand. If possible, the heels are rubbed dry.

Finally, the horse is led back to his stable calm and relaxed, but, not until the horse has perhaps rolled, or started nibbling at his hay (a titbit as a 'thank you' will also be appreciated), can the rider, with his mind at ease, set about cleaning his tack. The bit must always be washed thoroughly in clean water. It is a good idea to wipe over the leather parts of the bridle with a dry cloth; the stirrups and girth should always be cleaned where necessary, and the rest of the saddle should be checked over for dirt.

37
Every Beginner's Dream

38

When Can I Ride?

When does a beginner reach the stage where he can ride? Obviously, there is no simple answer to this question. We must first make clear what is meant by 'being able to ride'. Does it mean being able to sit on a horse more or less securely, or does it mean riding advanced dressage? When novice riders ask this question, what they nearly always mean is 'When can I start hacking out?'

Naturally, what every novice rider dreams of is riding through woods and fields; many riders never want to go beyond this, and derive a lot of pleasure from it. Some, however, become more interested in jumping or dressage, and only hack out occasionally, to give their horse a change of scenery and to let him relax. So when can a novice go out hacking for the first time? Basically, the answer to this is: when he is more or less capable of riding a quiet school horse on the aids with a more or less secure seat and has mastered the rein, leg and weight aids. Some people reach this stage in 15 lessons, others take much longer. On average, after about 30 hours in the school, a beginner should be able to go out hacking for the first time, in a group, and under the supervision of an instructor or experienced rider.

The rider should never rely on his own judgement and impressions to tell him when he is ready. It is impossible for a novice to imagine what dangers may be lying in wait for an inexperienced rider. Always wait until the instructor decides the time is right, and do not pester him. If you really cannot wait, discuss the matter with the instructor, and he will probably let you ride round in the grounds, or round and about outside the school, at the end of one of your lessons.

Hacking comprises a whole range of different experiences. Obviously, a novice rider does not start off with a ride lasting several hours. One hour is plenty for the first time. The terrain also make a difference, as does the pace at which it is ridden. An instructor who has the welfare of his students at heart will do a lot of walking to start with. He will familiarise them gradually with the skills of riding across country. The ground is rarely flat, there are ditches and small banks to be negotiated, and you sometimes have to ride downhill.

All this will show whether the basic training has been sound. Anyone who has learned, after a fashion, to stay 'on top', can gallop a horse flat out across a stubble field. It is quite another matter to ride across difficult terrain while still keeping the horse steady and on the aids.

Of course, this training does not end when the rider goes for his first ride outside; far from it. The first hack is just a marker to aim for, and it is also a sort of yardstick against which the instructor can check how well each student has assimilated his early riding lessons.

Conclusion

For six years you have struggled to learn the vocabulary of some foreign language, and finally the time comes for your first holiday in the country concerned. How disillusioned you feel when you cannot understand a word! You must learn the rules, and the basic principles are the first stage in every course of training, but it does make things easier if the everyday jargon is also learned from the outset. This is what this book sets out to teach. No novice rider who reads this book will then be qualified to go out and ride advanced dressage. No one should use this book like an instruction booklet to try to teach himself to ride from scratch, without an instructor. Yet this book, as an accompaniment to the early riding lessons, will make it much easier for a novice to gain entry into the world of horses, horsey people and riding. It does not reject the important and irrefutable rules and principles of horsemanship. What it does try to do is to present the training and the process of developing the beginnings of a secure seat in the saddle, as it takes place in practice.

It is the author's opinion that it serves little purpose to explain the perfect way to do things, while forgetting that in horsemanship, of all things, you can never achieve perfection. The author considers that minor weaknesses have their place, even in an introductory volume for beginners. A high value is placed in this book on the approximate comparisons and explanations. The rider will learn plenty about the leg aids, hands and school figures, even if his trainer is not particularly high powered. However, what he does not usually learn is why he uses many of the aids. This is because the trainer cannot explain the theory behind them. This volume, which is a genuine instruction book for beginners, has this as its primary objective. It should prove a staunch ally in the difficult early days, or serve to explain the theory behind something which has already been learned in practice.

If this book has made it possible for the novice rider to be more at ease and less intimidated during his early lessons and his early contacts with other riders, then it has fulfilled its aim.